"Shane Snow and Joe Lazauskas spend the overwhelming majority of their time thinking, writing, and theorizing about brand storytelling - so you don't have to. They're smart and they know this topic inside out (and sideways). Read their book. While I can't guarantee you'll rise to Shane and Joe's ridiculously obsessive level, you will be infinitely better prepared to tell your own brand's story. Promise!"

—**Rebecca Lieb**, analyst, author, advisor

"The Contently team understands the power of story, and how to craft and spread a great narrative, like no other. In an era where brand, design, and mission are a competitive advantage for every business, Contently underscores the importance of stories and how they transform companies and industries."

—**Scott Belsky**, entrepreneur, investor, founder of Behance, and bestselling author of *Making Ideas Happen*

"I can't think of a better way to illustrate the power of storytelling than by telling great stories. This book should be required reading not just by those with content in their titles, but by anyone in Marketing AND Sales. Then, when you're done, give it to your CEO to read . . . but make sure you get it back, because I guarantee you'll refer to it more than once."

—**Shawna Dennis**, senior marketing leader

"When it comes to storytelling edge, Joe and Shane have it—they're among the best minds in the business on the subject of content-centric marketing. Their book is a must-read for anyone looking to create profitable and sustainable relationships with customers. Basically, everyone."

—**Margaret Magnarelli**, senior director of marketing and managing editor of content, Monster

THE
STORYTELLING
EDGE

JOE LAZAUSKAS | SHANE SNOW

CONTENTLY PRESENTS

THE

STORYTELLING

EDGE

HOW TO TRANSFORM YOUR BUSINESS,

STOP SCREAMING INTO THE VOID,

AND MAKE PEOPLE LOVE YOU

WILEY

For general information on our other products and services or for technical support, please contact our Customer Care Department within the United States at (800) 762-2974, outside the United States at (317) 572-3993 or fax (317) 572-4002.

Wiley publishes in a variety of print and electronic formats and by print-on-demand. Some material included with standard print versions of this book may not be included in e-books or in print-on-demand. If this book refers to media such as a CD or DVD that is not included in the version you purchased, you may download this material at http://booksupport.wiley.com. For more information about Wiley products, visit www.wiley.com.

ISBN 978-1-119-48335-9 (Hardcover)
ISBN 978-1-119-48340-3 (ePDF)
ISBN 978-1-119-48347-2 (ePub)

Printed in the United States of America

10 9 8 7 6 5 4 3 2

To Charlie and Lighthouse and all the other Contently OGs.

CONTENTS

ACKNOWLEDGMENTS

This book is a product of years of work by all the good, brilliant, and delightful people of Contently. There are too many people to thank by name. Shout-out to Daniel Broderick and Ryan Galloway for edits and fact-checking. Shout-out to Kristen, Dillon, Erin, Kieran, Eunmo, Judy, Cynthia, Elisa, Ari, KP, Rebecca Lieb, and the rest of the TCS/Quarterly/ Strategy gang whose work has been the backbone of all of this. Special thanks to Sam for taking all the bullets for us, Kelly for mentorship and air cover, and, of course, to Joe and Dave for making it all possible. Thanks for Jim and Jeanenne for believing in this project. Super, extra big shout-out to Contently's unsung hero, Jordan Teicher, and our girl Jess @ Contently, who helped us shape the speeches and stories that make up so much of this book.

As a good Jewish boy, Joe thanks his mom, dad, and nana for all the support, and never trying too hard to talk him out of this "writer phase." Props to Mr. V for the tough love, Sam Apple for getting him into the game, and the group chat for listening to us talk about content strategy so much and still being our friends.

ABOUT THE AUTHORS

Joe Lazauskas is a New Jersey native. Shane Snow is an Idahoan. Both are New Yorkers now. Joe has written for *Fast Company*, *Forbes*, Mashable, and many more. Shane has written for *GQ*, *Wired*, *The New Yorker*, and others. Shane cofounded Contently in late 2010, and Joe joined soon after as editor in chief.

Learn more about Contently, Inc. at:

WWW.CONTENTLY.COM

Subscribe to the Content Strategist at:

WWW.CONTENTLY.COM/SUBSCRIBE

INTRODUCTION

A few years ago, a pale woman with crazy eyebrows and a keytar strapped to her back shot a home video. Standing on a street corner in Melbourne, Australia, at dusk, she wore a kimono and held up Sharpied signs. One by one, the signs flipped. They explained that the woman had spent the past four years writing songs. She was a musician. She had parted ways with her record label, which wanted to charge an outrageous amount to produce her next album. She and her bandmates were happy to no longer be with the label, and they had worked hard to create some great new music and art. But they couldn't finish producing the record on their own. If their new business—independent music—was going to get off the ground, they needed people's help.

"This is the future of music," one of her signs read. Another: "I love you."

Then she posted the video on the crowdfunding website Kickstarter.

In 30 days, the video raised $1.2 million—more than 10 times her goal. Nearly 25,000 people preordered the album, bought artwork, or simply donated money. The album and tour became a huge success, and the artist turned her music into a profitable business.

The woman in the kimono was named Amanda Palmer. She changed the game for independent musicians with that campaign. And she didn't do it by asking for money.

She did it by telling her story.

Stories Matter

Every few minutes, a new buzzword rips through the business world, gets a bunch of blog posts written about it, and ends up in a pile of tired terms next to "*synergy*." Today, one of the biggest corporate buzzwords is "*storytelling*." Marketers are obsessed with storytelling. Conference panels on the subject have fewer empty seats than *Hamilton* on Broadway.

Funny thing is, storytelling has been the buzzword off and on since the advent of advertising. It keeps rising to the top of the pile because it's timeless. Stories have driven human behavior throughout history—for good and for ill.

And in the digital age, businesses, workers, and leaders have more opportunities than ever to stand out, spread their message, and spark change through stories.

Good stories surprise us. They make us think and feel. They stick in our minds and help us remember ideas and concepts in a way that a PowerPoint crammed with bar graphs never can.

Stories are the reason thousands of creators like Amanda Palmer have rallied the support of millions on Kickstarter, and Kickstarter knows this. It doesn't just allow creators to tell their story; it requires it. Every project must have a video in which the creators explain what they're doing and why they need help.

As Internet, mobile messaging, and sharing tools transform our lives, storytelling is becoming an essential skill in any job. As we spend more and more time-consuming information by the streamful, storytelling is a core skill that every business—and individual—will need to master.

Unfortunately, in the era of PowerPoints and status updates, many of us have forgotten how to tell a good story.

Businesses Need to Tell Good Stories

Recent research indicates that 78 percent of chief marketing officers at big companies think that content—which is to say information, entertainment, education, and in an ideal world comes in the form of or is a piece of a story—is the future of their job. Two-thirds of brand marketers think that content is better than most types of advertising. That's huge.

This is largely because social media has gotten us comfortable conversing with anyone and any company. It's now commonplace to find "brand content" in our Facebook streams next to pictures of our loved ones and stories from the *New York Times*. As the majority of corporations present themselves as publishers, the defining characteristic of success will be the ability to not only put things on the Internet, but also craft compelling stories.

The fact is no one really loves being interrupted with a sales pitch. But everyone likes a good story. The businesses that can tell a good story today (and there are some really good ones right now) will have an advantage tomorrow.

Workers and Leaders Need to Tell Good Stories

All things being equal, people with powerful "personal brands"—that is, great reputations—have a leg up on getting jobs and being promoted to leadership roles. And personal brands are built on the stories we tell and the stories that are told about us.

Stories make presentations better. Stories make ideas stick. Stories help us persuade people. Savvy leaders tell stories to inspire and motivate us. (That's why so many politicians tell stories in their speeches, and many have backgrounds as authors and entertainers.)

And like Amanda Palmer's story endeared her to tens of thousands of strangers, our own stories can help us build our businesses and careers, too. Sure, we need science and data to make the right decisions in life and work, but the best business books and keynote speakers use stories to help us remember their ideas even when their stat slides fade from our memory.

Who Are We?

We're two journalists who care a lot about storytelling and what it means for the future of business.

Shane graduated from Columbia Journalism School when the media world was in crisis. Thanks to the fast-changing economics of media and the greatest recession in a century, newspapers and magazines were hemorrhaging jobs at a historic rate. Shane saw his talented classmates face dwindling full-time job prospects and struggle to even find decent freelance work.

At the same time, after years of hustling as a freelance journalist himself, Joe was trying to keep his digital news startup, The Faster Times, afloat despite fast-falling advertising rates.

Both of us saw the same opportunity: Social media was completely changing the dynamics of marketing and advertising for businesses. It allowed brands to reach people directly, like never before. To capitalize on that opportunity, brands would need something that they didn't have: great storytellers.

So, in 2010, Shane teamed up with his childhood friend from Idaho, an Internet entrepreneur named Joe Coleman, and an engineer buddy named Dave Goldberg to create Contently, which helped broker gigs for freelance journalists to write blogs and social media content for brands. Simultaneously, Joe was building his own network of writers and helping brands get content programs off the ground.

A little over a year later, we joined forces, and Joe became Contently's editor in chief. Contently grew into a thriving technology company with a suite of software that helps Fortune 500 companies (and others) to create, manage, and optimize content to build relationships with employees and customers. We wanted to give brands the tools to tell stories that people love, and measure the impact those stories had on their bottom line—what we call "engaging and accountable content."

Contently became the preeminent technology company in the emerging field of content marketing. And our blog, *The Content Strategist*, became the daily news of the content industry, with millions of readers. As Shane likes to say, we were in the water when a huge wave came, and we surfed it.

We are fundamentally nerds. In our years together at Contently, we've become obsessed with not only the art of storytelling for business but also the psychology and neuroscience of how stories actually transform human relationships. That obsession produced this book.

Throughout the book, we're going to speak in the first person a lot. Some of the stories we share happened to one of us or the other. Most of the time, though, we're just going to use the royal "we" for simplicity. If it helps, you can imagine that we're wearing a gigantic shirt with two heads coming out of it. (This is actually what we are doing right now. It's part of our creative process. Don't judge.)

Why This Book?

If you're reading this book, you've probably heard of content marketing, brand publishing, brand storytelling, or one of its many euphemisms.

The Internet has a glut of content about content. There's plenty of people preaching that we should do storytelling for marketing. The thing we found, though, is that there's a distinct lack of material on what we think is the most important part:

How does great storytelling actually work?

And how can a business actually get better at it?

At Contently, we preach that content is more than a marketing tactic. We believe that great stories are the secret weapon that can make every part of a business better.

Storytelling helps people remember you. It gives businesses an edge when it comes to hiring. It helps salespeople get in doors, bolsters a company's reputation, and can help everyone within an organization be more connected and informed. We believe that weaving stories into our products, services, presentations, and habits can change everything about how we work, live, and do business.

In this book, we'll show how to make all that happen.

There's a Native American proverb on our office wall that says, "Those who tell the stories rule the world." As technology increasingly intertwines us, we believe that's increasingly true. It's our job as businesses, workers, and leaders to make sure the good guys are the ones telling the best stories.

As Amanda Palmer might write with her Sharpie: This is the future of business. We love you. And we want to give you an edge.

1 The Power of Story

P retend that the world decided to elect a queen. The candidates have been whittled down to two well-known British women: Queen Elizabeth and J. K. Rowling, author of the Harry Potter series.

You have been asked to vote in this election based on who you trust more. Who would you vote for, and why?

A couple of years ago we were curious about this, so we took the geeky route and asked 3,000 Americans this question.

The results of our election might surprise you.

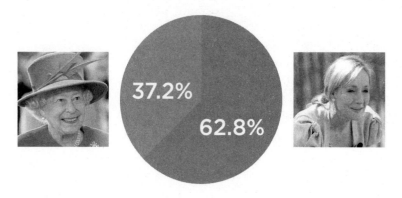

37.2%

62.8%

Rowling, the children's book author, beat Elizabeth, the monarch, by what pollsters call a landslide.

But why?

Why would we be more likely to trust the author over the queen? Why would we choose the storyteller over the woman with a lifetime of leadership experience? And what does this have to do with the business world?

In this book, we're going to answer those questions. First, we'll dig into the science of story and what stories do to our brains. Then we'll get into how we can become powerful storytellers ourselves and how to use storytelling as a strategy to persuade and present more effectively at work, grow our businesses, and make a difference in the world.

And, as you might have guessed, we're going to start with a couple of stories.

Jacques and the Beggar

Many years ago, a French poet named Jacques Prévert was walking down the street. He passed a beggar asking for money. For whatever reason, Jacques decided to stop and talk to the man.

"How's it going?" Jacques asked.

As the beggar turned, Jacques noticed that he was blind. In fact, he had a sign that said so.

The beggar replied, "It's not going very well. People walk by and they don't leave any money in my hat. Would you give me some money?"

"I'm a poor writer," Jacques said. "I have no money. But perhaps I could rewrite your sign for you?"

"By all means," said the beggar. He had nothing to lose.

So Jacques took the sign, flipped it over, and wrote a new message. And then he went about his day.

A few days later, Jacques was walking along the same path, came across the same beggar, and decided to ask the same question.

"How's it going?"

This time the beggar's tune had changed.

"People have been so generous lately," he said. "My hat fills up three times a day. Thank you, thank you for what you wrote on my sign."

Here's what Jacques had written:

"Spring is coming, but I won't see it."

With one sentence, Jacques transformed a statement into a story. In a single line, he changed a man's life.

Now—keep that story in the back of your mind while we tell you one of Shane's favorite stories in the world:

And Now for Shane's Favorite Ryan Gosling Story

Ryan Gosling is an actor. He's pretty.

For a long time, Shane didn't care about him at all.

Sure, he seemed like a good actor. But Shane never saw *The Notebook*, which the whole world adored. He knew there was a bizarre amount of Internet meme activity around Gosling. But, you know, whatever. He was okay.

Then one day, Shane was sitting in the audience of a business conference. Some guy was giving a terribly dull presentation—one of those talks where there are about 250 words of tiny text crammed onto every single slide. Shane ran out of emails to answer, so he began browsing Wikipedia. We don't quite know how, but at some point, he ended up on the entry for Ryan Gosling. And for whatever reason, he decided to go ahead and read it.

Don't judge. As we said, the presentation was really boring.

Here's the gist of Ryan's story, according to the editors at Wikipedia:

Gosling had a bit of a sad childhood. He grew up in Canada. (That was not the sad part!) His dad was a traveling salesman, so his family moved a lot. When he was young, his parents split up. He ended up living with his mom, who worked full time. All the moving and family trouble affected him. He had a hard time making friends. He didn't learn to read until far later than most kids—nearly into his teens. He was diagnosed with ADHD.

Watching television became Gosling's favorite hobby. He loved movies and accents. He loved *The Mickey Mouse Club*. He loved Marlon Brando.

But he was bullied at school. Moving around and watching a lot of TV probably didn't help him make friends.

Things came to a head one day at school when he brought knives to primary school and threw them at the kids who bullied him. He'd decided to take matters into his own hands like his action film hero Rambo.

Around age 12, Gosling begged his mom to let him go to an audition for *The Mickey Mouse Club* in Montreal. He was a cute, talented kid, and he got the part.

Now here's the crazy part of the story: Because his mother couldn't move to Orlando with him, Gosling got adopted by none other than Justin Timberlake's mom. (Or rather, she became his legal guardian.)

He learned how to perform on *The Mickey Mouse Club*. He learned to read well. He learned to focus. He grew up.

. . . and he became Ryan Gosling.

And then something strange happened.

After reading this Wikipedia entry, Shane suddenly wanted to watch some Ryan Gosling movies. So he went and watched *The Notebook*. (Turns out it's fantastic!) The next time a Gosling movie was in the theater, Shane watched it. He started telling people about how cool Ryan Gosling was. How human he was. It wasn't long before people started introducing him as, "This is Shane—he founded Contently, and he's a HUGE Ryan Gosling fan."

And it was true! Ten minutes on Wikipedia had turned him from apathetic to advocate. He's on Team Gosling, and he's on it simply because he learned his story.

As weird as it sounds, Shane feels like he has a relationship with Ryan.

We learn a couple of things from these two stories. First: Stories are powerful. Both Jacques's experience with the blind man and Shane's with Ryan Gosling show this. They illustrate what great stories fundamentally do: They build relationships, and they make people care.

People didn't care much about the blind man when he asked for money. But when he helped people understand what it was like to be in his shoes—when he shared his story—they were moved to help him.

Shane didn't care about Ryan Gosling. Now he refers to him by his first name. If they ever meet, he's going to give Ryan a hug. But we bet Ryan's used to that sort of thing by now.

This power of stories to change our minds, to build relationships and make people care, is more than just neat. It's scientific.

A few years ago, a group of researchers from University of Pennsylvania gave $5 to random people and asked them to read different letters from charities asking for money. When the plea for donations relied on statistics and talked about widespread problems, people donated less. When the request involved a story of an individual in pain, people donated more.

Versions of this experiment have been repeated dozens of times using television commercials, brochures, and in-person persuasion. The result is always the same. A plea for help will get some donations. But a story always gets more.

That's because . . .

Our Brains Are Built for Story

In the classic tale *In the Heart of the Sea: The Tragedy of the Whaleship Essex* by Nathaniel Philbrick, a group of sailors were "zagging" off the coast of South America in 1821 when they came across something ghastly. They were in a whaling ship named the *Dauphin*, under the command of a captain named Zimri Coffin. One day on the horizon a small boat popped into view in the middle of the ocean. Here's an account of what the Dauphin crew saw:

> Under Coffin's watchful eye, the helmsman brought the ship as close as possible to the derelict craft. Even though their momentum quickly swept them past it, the brief

seconds during which the ship loomed over the open boat presented a sight that would stay with the crew the rest of their lives . . .

First they saw bone—human bones—littering the thwarts and floorboards, as if the whaleboat were the seagoing lair of a ferocious man-eating beast.

Then they saw the two men.

They were curled up in opposite ends of the boat, their skin covered with sores, their eyes bulging from the hollows of their skulls, their beards caked with salt and blood. They were sucking the marrow from the bones of their dead shipmates.[1]

Quick! Think about where you were when you just read that. Do you recall how the seat you were sitting in felt as you pictured the salt-caked beards of the cannibal shipmates? Did someone in the room with you happen to cough while you read this? Do you recall any background noises outside? Any trucks or sirens?

By the time you finished reading that passage, chances are your brain had pulled you into the story. Your imagination filled in the scene, and your present circumstances faded into the background of your consciousness. This is what Jonathan Gottschall, who shares this anecdote in his wonderful book *The Storytelling Animal*, calls "the witchery of story." It's what our brains have been biologically programmed to do.

We are hardwired to dramatize, to imagine, and to be pulled into good stories. Think about the last time you watched a movie or read a book and were suddenly snapped back to reality by a noise in the room. You hadn't realized that you'd lost awareness of your surroundings. You didn't notice when the line between reality and the story world inside your brain began to fade. That process—which we go through every night while we sleep—is a survival mechanism that helps us do a better job of storing information in our memory.

Stories Help Us Remember

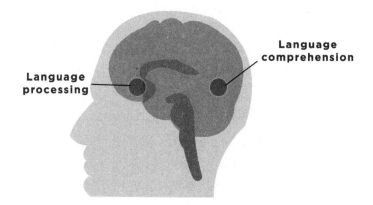

We also know the areas of your brain that light up when you hear or see a story:

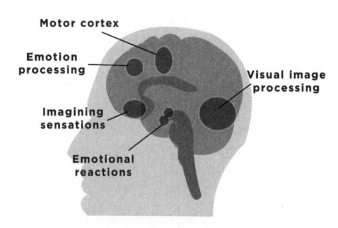

It turns out that something surprising happens when information comes via a story than via simple facts: More of our brains light up. When we hear a story, the neural activity increases fivefold, like a switchboard has suddenly illuminated the city of our mind.

Scientists have a saying: "Neurons that fire together, wire together." When more of your brain is at work at a given point of time, the chances that your brain will remember the work it did increases exponentially.

Pretend, for example, you are in high school health class, and your teacher is giving a slideshow presentation. The first slide features a chart filled with stats on how many people die or are ruined every year from drug use. The teacher says, "Drugs are dangerous."

In this moment, the areas of your brain responsible for language processing and comprehension will be working to absorb this information.

Now say that instead you have a substitute teacher who takes a different approach. She puts up a slide with a photograph of a handsome teenager. "This is Johnny," she says. "He was a good kid, but he had a lot of family problems that made it hard to be happy some days. He was quiet and got picked on a lot. So he started hanging out with some of the other picked-on kids. One day, one of them offered him drugs. He started doing lots of drugs to make himself feel better. Ten years later, he looked like this—" cut to a photograph of a sickly looking mid-20 s young man with missing teeth. And then, the teacher gives the same message as the first: "Drugs are dangerous."

During this lecture, all sorts of areas of your brain will be active. Areas that help you imagine what Johnny's life is like. How he feels. How you might feel some of the same things.

Unsurprisingly, the second kind of presentation—the story—is a lot more memorable. Students who see that presentation are going to be more likely to think about Johnny next time someone offers them drugs. No matter what choice they make, they are more likely to remember the message that drugs are dangerous.

Do you see where we're going? When we get information through stories, we engage more neurons. As a result, the story is wired into our memory much more reliably.

Imagine how this could change your next presentation.

Stories Generate Empathy—at the Chemical Level

A few years ago, scientists packed a bunch of people into a movie theater to see exactly how stories work on our brains. They put helmets on the participants' heads, strapped on monitors to measure their heart rate and breathing, and taped perspiration trackers onto their bodies. The participants looked around nervously, laughed as they made small talk, and fiddled with their helmet straps.

And then a James Bond movie began.

As the movie played, the scientists closely monitored the audience's physiological reaction. When James Bond found himself in stressful situations—like hanging from a cliff or fighting a bad guy—the audience's pulses raced. They sweated. Their attention focused.

And something else interesting happened: At the same time, their brains synthesized a neurochemical called oxytocin.

Oxytocin is our empathy drug. It sends us a signal that we should care about someone. In prehistoric times, this was useful for figuring out if a person that was approaching you was safe. Were they a friend, or were they going to club you on the head and steal your woolly mammoth steak? Through oxytocin, our brains helped us identify tribe members whom we should help survive. Because that would help us survive, too.

Our heart rates rise when James Bond is in danger because our brains have decided that he—this familiar character—is part of our tribe. We generate oxytocin when we see him, which makes us empathize with his story when we watch it. And, circularly, the more of his story we experience, the more oxytocin our brain secretes.

That means that we're not just watching James Bond. We're putting ourselves in his shoes. At the deepest physiological level, it means that we really care.

Oxytocin levels can actually predict how much empathy people will have for someone else.

And—fun fact!—there's actually now such a thing as synthetic oxytocin. You can shoot it into your nose like Flonase. One of the first thing scientists did with this, of course, was make people snort oxytocin and then ask them to give money to charity.

Perhaps you won't be surprised to learn that, compared to regular people, oxytocin snorters were more charitable. (Maybe some drugs aren't so bad!)

Stories Bring Us Together

It's hard to learn someone's story and not feel connected to them. The oxytocin we get from stories helps us care, whether we like it or not.

This is basically the premise of the film *The Breakfast Club*. A group of misfits is forced to come together for detention one Saturday. After sitting miserably for a while—hating each other—they start to share stories about their personal lives, their parents, and, of course, their dreams. Over the course of the movie, they form a bond. When they leave detention and go back to their different worlds, they remain closer than before. They aren't necessarily going to be best friends, but they now understand and respect one another. You can imagine them standing up for one another against a bully or becoming close friends after high school, when the artificial boundaries of their cliques start to disintegrate.

But even more interesting, we don't even need to share our own stories to build a relationship with someone. Sharing almost any story makes a difference. In a 2011 research study in New Zealand published in the *Journal of Teaching and Teacher Education*, researchers put kids from different racial and economic backgrounds together for a series of storytime activities. The scientists found that even when the kids weren't sharing their own stories—when they were simply reading storybooks—they developed empathy for one another. They felt more connected. And as they grew up, they were less racist and classist than other kids.

Storytelling, the researchers concluded, "fostered empathy, compassion, tolerance and respect for difference."[2]

This is why it makes sense that people still go on dates to the movies. On the surface, a movie is a terrible date. Both people experience the movie separately. It's a parallel activity that doesn't involve interacting with your date at all. And yet, it becomes a shared experience. Because your brain is wired to remember experiencing the movie's story more deeply and vividly than other experiences, that story becomes subconsciously more meaningful to you—even if the movie was bad. And the fact that you and your date experienced the same story together actually brings you closer.

This is another way storytelling played a part in how we survived as a human species. When we were first building civilization, we grouped up in tribes. We had this magnificent brain, but we had to protect it against saber-toothed tigers and poisonous berries and thousands of other things that could kill us at any moment. We had to work together to survive. We had to hunt together, gather food together, make shelter together, and pass on lessons that we learned so that our descendants would survive, too.

But how could we do that, when we didn't have a written language to record what we'd learned, how we'd survived? The answer, of course, was stories.

Evolutionary biologists say that the human brain developed the ability to tell stories—to imagine them and to dream them—around the same time as our ability to speak. Storytelling was an essential piece of the development and endurance of language.

And so we would gather as tribes at the end of our workday. We would take the wide world of stimuli from our time hunting and gathering and building. And we would package it all into stories—the stories that helped us remember and care.

Think for a minute about something you're particularly loyal to. Like your family, your country, or your favorite sports team. Our loyalty is often somewhat irrational. Our families may not always be that nice to be around. Our countries might not actually be giving us everything we need. Our favorite sports team might be the New York Jets.

Why might you love, say, a grandparent who lives so far away that you never see them? Or an uncle whose social and political views directly oppose yours? Aside from the fact that they probably love you, too, you've probably spent a lot of time at the dinner table or on the porch hearing interesting stories about them. Those stories strengthened your relationship, despite distance or differences.

Why do Americans love their country so much? At the time of this writing, the education and health systems are more expensive and rank lower than most developed countries. Job security is low; income inequality is high. We have more people in prison than any country in the world (and more per capita than every country except Seychelles, which, it turns out, has a big pirate problem). There's a lot of amazing things about the U. S. of A., but there's a lot that needs to be better, too. And yet Americans constantly talk about how it's "the greatest country in the world."

That's because we grow up hearing badass stories about the place. The story of America is truly a Hollywood tale, an underdog story about a cast of misfits who won an improbable battle for freedom against the most powerful empire on Earth. Those stories have left heroic images seared into our minds:

The Boston Tea Party sparking a thunderous display of defiance. The Founding Fathers urging on a revolutionary army with rags for boots. Washington sneaking across the icy Delaware River to launch a surprise attack that turned the tide of the war. Stories about Tesla, Einstein, and all the great inventors and innovators and pioneers who immigrated to America and made a difference.

Why might you love the Jets when they constantly let you down? Maybe you grew up hearing stories about them, too. (Joe Namath and his fur coat FTW!) Or you associate watching the drama of a Jets game—which unfolds as a story itself—with your parents, siblings, or college roommates. You've formed a bond through those stories—a bond that resists rationale. Whether that story is of the Butt Fumble or an improbable upset of the Patriots in the playoffs, it forms a bond that's incredibly difficult to break.

Those stories—and that bond—help you endure the tough times, so you can move forward together with your team or country (or whoever!) and not just abandon ship at the first sign of trouble. This is how humans have overcome obstacles together since we were living around campfires.

Research shows that families that spend dinnertime together end up having stronger relationships. That's in large part because of what we do at family dinner: We tell stories. We ask each other what happened. We reenact the comedies and the dramas of our day. And through sharing those stories, we build relationships of trust and care.

This is how religions impart messages, too. It's how, through stories, we remember the parables, the life lessons, the things that we need to do to be better people and take care of others. Stories are the bridge that connects our disparate lives.

Every great movement in history has used stories to inspire humans to come together around a cause. When we marched on Washington, DC, in 1963, thousands of people from different backgrounds linked arms because of the stories of Rosa Parks and others, stories that changed the way folks thought about civil rights—or made them care enough to fight for them.

When you look at the history of business, it should be no surprise that the kinds of companies that build the most loyalty are the ones for which storytelling is their business. They're the newspapers, magazines, movie studios, and television production companies that educate and entertain us every day with stories. They're so successful at getting and keeping people's attention through stories that brands pay them millions of dollars to advertise next to those stories.

These media companies teach us a lesson that all great businesses tomorrow need to know: If you want people to buy your product, you have to get them to care about your story.

In the late 2000s, for example, Ford Motor Company found itself in trouble when its cars were started to get a reputation as low quality. Foreign cars seemed to be getting better and better. Meanwhile, Fords were breaking down, people were disappointed, and sales were falling.

So Ford used stories to get people to care again. They took documentary film crews into the Ford factories and interviewed employees working on the assembly lines and designing the next generation of vehicles.

And they said to the cameras: We know that we have screwed up. We know that Ford isn't what it used to be, but we are all working hard to turn things around and to make our cars awesome again. So we're going to show you the stories of the people who are your neighbors, who are working on these cars, who are working to make this product once more the product that you know and love.

These stories helped Ford to clear the air with customers and get people to pay attention to them and their plans for the future. The series became a terrific early step in Ford's long journey to turning things around.

With Great Power . . .

As you can see, we're a little obsessed. Stories have done a lot of good throughout history. They've helped us survive. They've helped us build relationships and societies. They've helped us create movements and businesses. They're an essential part of what makes us human.

One day a few years ago we decided to conduct a study to replicate the effects of the Jacques Prévert and the beggar story. We found two homeless signs on Google Images and asked 3,000 people which one they would donate to if they had $1 to give. One sign was a sales pitch, a plea for help. The other sign was a story.

Of course, our hypothesis was that the story sign would make the most money. The question was just how much more effective would the sign be.

The results of the poll, however, caught us by surprise.

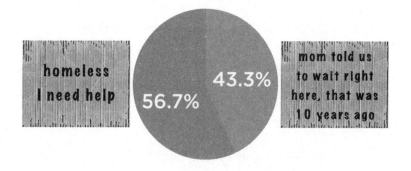

The sign that told a story didn't win.

But then we dug a little deeper. We had asked each survey respondent to explain why they picked their answer. Most of the people who picked Sign #1 did so for a telling reason.

They said they didn't pick Sign #1 because it was a better sign. They picked it because they didn't think Sign #2 was true.

Which, of course, it can't be. Nobody would wait for 10 years on a street corner for their mom. It's a sad sign, but it's also obviously a put-on. (In fact, many who voted for the story sign said they did so because they thought it was funny, not because they thought it was true!)

This illustrates an essential point. Whereas we humans are built for story, we're also built to discern. We look for things that are wrong. And despite all the power that stories have for good, a story that deceives people is likely to backfire.

We've talked a lot about how stories are used for good. But stories have been used in history for evil as well. Dictators throughout history have used stories to inspire fear and mistrust—to create loyalty through division and to make people believe in wrong and hateful ideas.

The good news is that, at the end of the day, if you're using stories for evil, the truth will come out. Eventually, citizens rebel. Those stories start to lose their credibility, and good people turn around to fight the deceivers.

As people and companies in the twenty-first century, we can't afford to be dishonest storytellers. We need to recognize that when we're using stories to build relationships, we can't lie. For stories to make a powerful and lasting impact, they have to be congruent. You can't post YouTube videos about protecting the environment while you're dumping sewage into the river out back.

That's not to say that we can't build relationships through fictional stories. People voted for J. K. Rowling in our Queen of the World poll even though her stories are make believe. That's okay, because we knew what we were getting when we picked up those Harry Potter books. Rowling's contract with us was that she would tell us an incredible, fictional story about a school of wizards. She fulfilled that. She was congruent.

Which brings us back to the question that opened this chapter. Why would we trust the storyteller over the monarch? Why did we vote J.K. over Queen Elizabeth? In our poll's comments, people by and large said, "I feel like I know her."

And, indeed, we did get to know her. Over seven books and thousands of pages, we learned what she cares about, how she thinks, and whom she loves. We had empathy for her characters, who reminded us of people we care about in our own lives. And in the background, our brains were at work, firing and wiring and oxytocin-*ing* like crazy.

Now that we understand why stories work, for the rest of this book, we're going to talk about how to make them work. Because what good is a story if you don't know how to tell it?

2 The Elements of Great Storytelling

W e would have never gotten *Star Wars* if the Modesto, California, police weren't so good at their job. Or if George Lucas wasn't such a reckless driver.

Before he became a filmmaker and the beloved creator of *Star Wars*, Lucas wanted to be a fighter pilot in the U.S. Air Force. But they wouldn't let him in because he had too many speeding tickets.

His backup plan was film school. And thus, after a decade of work and innumerable headaches, we got *Star Wars*—a story that every person on Planet Earth has heard something about. (In his book *How Star Wars Conquered the Universe*, author Chris Taylor visited all sorts of remote tribes attempting to find an adult human being who had not in some way been affected by *Star Wars*–and couldn't find even one!)

Star Wars has something for everyone. Even if you happen to be a horrible person (or, you know, not just that into sci-fi) and dislike *Star Wars*, it still has at least one thing for you—a template for what we have dubbed The Four Elements of Great Stories.

Element 1: Relatability

There's something innately human and entertaining about the *Star Wars* adventures, but if you want to truly understand what made the first film so popular, you need to appreciate the culture in which it came to life.

America in the 1970s was fresh off its big victory versus Russia in the race to land on the moon. It was also an unsettling time in the world, with the Vietnam War, civil unrest, and a lot of bad disco music. Americans were nostalgic for "the good ol' days" of carefree 1950s culture, muscle cars, and skinny Elvis.

George Lucas was a big fan of 1950s car culture and nostalgic Americana. When you look at the first *Star Wars* film, his love of fast, roaring mechanical machines rips through the screen. And so does his love for a few other things, including comic books, kung fu movies, and old Buck Rogers science-fiction adventures.

Lucas took all of these things that he loved—that 1970s America loved—and mashed them all together to make *Star Wars*. The mask that Darth Vader wears was modeled after a kung fu helmet, and his stormtroopers were inspired by a kung fu army. The speeders looked like muscle cars, and the spaceships resembled something NASA might soon build. The costumes could've been from Buck Rogers, and the storyline was taken straight from Joseph Campbell's concept of the Hero's Journey (which we'll get into a bit later).

In other words, *Star Wars* is a universe constructed with a combination of a whole bunch of familiar things. Even though it was about space creatures living a long time ago in a galaxy far, far away, it captured the first and perhaps most important element of great stories: relatability.

Our brains are averse, so to speak, to things that are too foreign. It's hard to get comfortable enough to invest in a story that is too out there.

Conversely, we are fascinated by stories that we can relate to. Basically, we're a giant planet of narcissists.

For us to accept the unfamiliar parts of *Star Wars*—like a space bar filled with aliens brawling—we need some familiar things to get us comfortable and make us care. And the more relatable a story is, the more likely we are to get pulled in.

BuzzFeed, for example, has managed to capture millions of people's attention through stories by specifically playing on our love of relatability.

Take a typical BuzzFeed headline, like "25 Things You'll Understand If You Grew Up With Asian Parents." We didn't grow up with Asian parents, but when we saw this story, we forwarded it to an Asian American friend of ours who then laughed and forwarded it to everyone she knew. Millions of people ended up reading this story because a certain group— Asian kids and their friends—could relate to it so deeply that they had to check it out.

They do the same thing with colleges. BuzzFeed is filled with posts such as "21 Things That Could Only Happen at Stanford." They repeat this formula for almost every college in the country. And that's because they know that students who went to Stanford will share that video on Facebook, and the post will go viral among current students and alumni.

One of the secrets to BuzzFeed and a lot of the modern Internet's successful viral sites is they don't try to speak to everyone in every story; they try to relate very deeply to specific identity groups and bet that those groups will share these stories prolifically.

This is why character-driven stories are so powerful and why the characters that tend to be our favorites are the ones that resemble our loved ones or ourselves.

Part of what made *Star Wars* so great was its ensemble of colorful characters to root for: The kid with humble upbringing and big dreams. The smart and sarcastic princess. The rogue with the heart of gold. The bickering robot couple C-3PO and R2-D2, and whatever Wookiees are supposed to be. We had empathy for these characters. We saw something in them. We cared about them.

Interestingly, there's a concept in psychology that explains the appeal to the villains in *Star Wars*, too. Even though we might hate the bad guy in a story, the villains that fascinated us are the ones that we can see a little bit of ourselves in.

Psychologist Carl Jung calls this our "shadow." His research shows that we tend to loathe people who embody the things that we don't like about ourselves.

This explains what makes Darth Vader great. He was a good guy who went really, really bad. When we learn his story, we subconsciously see the badness that we fight within ourselves. That makes us counterintuitively love this villain, even though we might not be rooting for him.

This also explains why the original 1970s *Star Wars* movies were so beloved, and why the 2015 installment, *Star Wars: Episode VII—The Force Awakens*, received much more critical acclaim than the three prequel episodes released in the 1990s.

The 1990s movies had so many new characters and elements introduced that they felt too foreign. Jar Jar, Grievous, Dooku—we got too many new storylines, too fast, all at once. And the nostalgia that they tried to put into those movies felt too forced; it wasn't relatable because it wasn't natural. The clumsy backstory of the child Anakin building C-3PO—the very robot that would randomly end up being involved in stealing plans for grown-up Anakin's Death Star superweapon—wasn't nostalgic irony. It was corny.

In *The Force Awakens*—the seventh episode of the *Star Wars* saga, released in 2015—Lucasfilm brought back old characters, old themes, and plot lines that mimicked the originals. Even though many critics said it was too much like the originals, we collectively paid a billion dollars to see it.

It's a great reminder that stories that we latch onto are the ones that connect us to something in our past.

Element 2: Novelty

When you put someone's head under a scanner and show them something they've never seen before, the brain lights up. Much more, in fact, than when you show the person something it has seen before.

This is because our brains are wired for novelty. In evolutionary terms, we pay attention to what's new because we need to determine whether the new thing is a threat. Once again, this is part of how we survived.

Of course, something too new or completely foreign has the potential to scare us. Our brains get on high alert when they encounter novelty. They prepare to fight or flee.

The best stories use relatability to get us invested and then use novelty to keep us interested. They get the audience comfortable in the beginning, usually through a character or setting or scenario that we may care about, and then introduce novelty—the fun part—into the plot.

Think back to *Star Wars* again.

We start with Luke Skywalker in his humble beginnings, stuck doing routine work as a moisture farmer on a boring desert planet—and suddenly he gets thrust into an adventure. As the adventure proceeds, we delve into more and more foreign territory. And that's exciting.

Maintaining a balance of relatability and novelty is crucial. If we dive into novelty too quickly, we get the 1990s *Star Wars* films, where so much new stuff is going on that we found ourselves asking, "Why should I care?" as often as we asked, "What is even happening?"

Similarly, if a story doesn't have enough novelty, it will lose our attention.

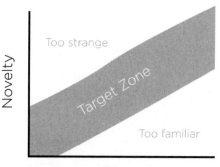

Now, you might be wondering: If novelty is so key to great stories, why does Hollywood crank out so many sequels?

We wondered the same thing. Was there something we were missing? Does the relatability of the original movies outweigh the novelty of doing something different?

We took a painstaking look at the performance of 600 recent movie sequels to find out.

(Get ready for a nerdy diversion!)

What Movie Popularity Data Tell Us about Novelty

Hollywood's first movie sequel, *The Fall of a Nation*, came out 100 years ago. Studios have pumped out sequels in earnest ever since. Some have done well, like *The Godfather Part II*, which won a Best Picture Oscar in 1974, and *The Empire Strikes Back*, which smashed box office records in 1980. This encouraged even more sequel making.

Fast-forward to 2016, and we'd already had a dozen sequels, including *Zoolander 2*, *Ride Along 2*, *Crouching Tiger Hidden Dragon 2*, *SLC Punk 2*, *IP Man 3*, and *Kung Fu Panda 3* between New Year's and the time the snow melted in New York. By November that year, theaters had shown 35 major sequels.

Interestingly, a quarter of the big sequels of 2016 were released over a decade after the first installments premiered. The number of these late sequels grows each year, hinting that movie studios are either hard up for original ideas or increasingly see sequels as good investments.

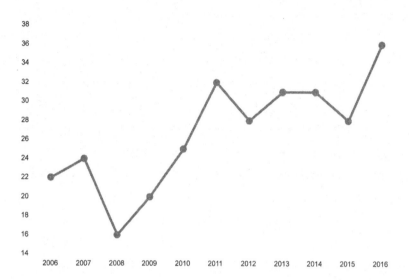

So are sequels better than originals? The premise of this section is that novelty wins, so we'd assume the answer to that question would be no. But why then do we keep making them?

The most common stat cited for movie success is box office earnings. There are two problems with using ticket sales as proxy for quality, though. First, the films nominated for Best Picture by the Academy are never the highest earners. Most winners don't crack the top 50.

But let's put that aside for a moment.

The bigger problem is that earnings are often a function of marketing. A larger budget—say, for a sequel to a film that earned a lot of money—may very well yield a big box office number. Spending more on big sequels is a rather safe bet. But ticket sales show that despite bigger budgets, the profits for sequels tend to continually fall. Even though spending more to promote a movie should make the movie more successful in theory, a greater budget often doesn't result in greater net profits.

Let's zoom out to the 600 sequels we catalogued (every sequel from 2006 to 2016, plus a few hundred sequels from previous decades). The first sequel in a series grosses more money, on average, than the original—though as the above analysis shows, that doesn't mean sequels have bigger profits. The second sequel of a franchise tends to make less money than the first sequel. Reboots, like 2009's *Star Trek*, typically earn more money than their predecessors.

These, however, are averages, skewed by a few exceptional cases. When we look at the median, we find that the typical sequel, including remakes, make dramatically less money in theaters than the original.

Twenty to 40 percent less, in fact!

Even though sequels usually make less money than their predecessors, they still make a lot more money than the average movie.

How does this work? If sequels are typically worse than their originals, why would sequels on a given year make more money than originals? The data actually tell the story quite nicely: Sequels only get made when the first movie is a huge success.

While the chances of making a hit original movie are small, chances are good that a sequel based on an existing hit will get attention.

In the movie business, sequels are just safer bets.

However, as we mentioned before, dollars do not necessarily correlate to quality. Let's take a look at how viewers feel about sequels after they've bought their tickets.

AVERAGE IMDB REVIEW SCORES OF MOVIE SEQUELS, BY YEAR

(HOW MUCH SEQUEL FILMS EACH YEAR WERE LIKED COMPARED TO THEIR ORIGINALS)

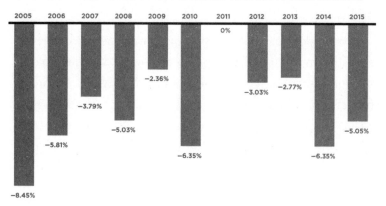

The story here is clear: We like sequels less than originals. We may pay to see sequels, but we don't like a rehashed film as much as a fresh one. This is so accepted in Hollywood that the entire plot of 2014's *22 Jump Street*, the sequel to *21 Jump Street*, is a self-referential allusion to the idea that a sequel just replicates the same story over again. In other words, the repeat-the-original system of sequels has become so cemented in Hollywood that an entire film was extremely successful by poking fun at this idea.

But what about the outliers? Sequels such as *The Return of the King* and *The Force Awakens* that blow us away as much or more than their originals? When you zoom in on the outliers, you'll notice that sequels tend to fall into two distinct categories. The bottom-performing sequels are essentially repeats— similar plots, similar jokes, basically 90 minutes of nostalgia. But the top-performing sequels tend to build on a strong storyline. They're not sequels; they're sagas.

It turns out that sequels that are part of sagas are enjoyed just as much as their predecessors. Their ratings are just as good as the originals. And reboots often get even more favorable reviews than the older versions. We like the newness! It's just the repeats we don't like.

A recent study on innovation by professors from the Universities of South Florida, Binghamton, Texas San Antonio, Münster, and Lausanne explains why we tend to like the continuing storylines of sagas better than repeats. The researchers concluded that people prefer ongoing storylines that mix the safety of familiar characters with the excitement of a fresh adventure. In other words, we want novelty, but we need relatability.

The best stories, according to the research, carefully balance that dynamic over time. When things change too much, the audience revolts. But when things stay the same, the audience gets bored.

Our biggest movies tend to break new ground—*Gone with the Wind*, *Citizen Kane*, *Star Wars*, *Jurassic Park*, and *Avatar*. If you're making a movie, you may indeed make money by making something unoriginal, but people won't like it. In the storytelling business, novelty creates the biggest winners.

Element 3: Tension

There's a scene at the beginning of the movie *Mission: Impossible III* where Ethan Hunt, the hero played by actor Tom Cruise, is tied to a chair. He's in terrible trouble. The bad guy has a gun to Hunt's wife's head and is counting to 10, telling him to give him information, or he will pull the trigger.

"Where is the rabbit's foot?!"

"I don't know!!!" Hunt is frantic.

The bad guy counts all the way up to 10, and then the screen goes blank.

And then the movie goes back in time to months earlier, to the adventure that led to Hunt being tied to that chair.

When Shane saw *MI3* for the first time, he had to pee at the beginning of the movie—and he ended up holding it because of this scene. There was no way he was going to miss what happened.

And that story—the one of Shane not peeing—illustrates something extremely powerful. It's the third element of terrific storytelling: tension. Some people call it the conflict, others call it the curiosity gap. Whatever you call it, tension is what turns a good story into a great story.

The greatest stories in history have it: the emotional tug, the mystery, the what-if, the "I can't believe this!" This element is what keeps us glued to our seat, no matter how badly we have to pee.

If we were to write the worst love story ever, it would probably go like this: "Jack and Jill grew up in houses next to each other. They were friends since they were kids. They decided to get married because, well, why not? It made sense. The families knew each other. And everyone was fine."

If we saw that movie in the theater, we would pee whenever we felt like it, and also ask for our money back. There's no tension. There's no hardship, there's no drama, and everything was just . . . fine. Boring.

The opposite of a boring love story is Romeo and Juliet. This classic story works because there's so much working against the characters. Their families hate each other. They have to keep their love secret, and they're willing to die for each other so that they can be together. Many things can go wrong—and so much does. All that tension makes the story extremely powerful.

Long before *Star Wars*, Aristotle described how tension makes a great story. He said that a great story establishes what is and then establishes what could be. The gap between those two things is the tension, and that is your story. The storyteller's job is to close that gap and open a new one, over and over until the tale is done.

Star Wars, of course, is full of tension. Even though it's a family franchise, it's not a peaceful ride.

The villains are family members. They blow up planets. Someone you love dies in nearly every episode of *Star Wars*. And this is what makes the story good. You don't know what's going to happen. You don't know who's going to make it. The characters want things so badly and are against such great odds that you have to keep watching. No one has ever gotten up to pee during the Death Star assault scene.

And at the end of each film, we smile.

Even the cliffhanger endings end on a note that makes our brains happy. We let out that sigh of relief, and our heart rates calm down when that orchestra plays and the end credits float through space.

The tension in *Star Wars* helps keep us in that place where our real world doesn't exist, where our brains fire neurochemicals to help us empathize with the characters.

Which is, of course, what storytelling is all about.

Element 4: Fluency

Some time ago, we were talking with some friends about how to become better writers. How could we write more intelligently? How could we increase the sophistication of our work?

Out of curiosity, we put some of our writing through an automated reading level calculator. We were surprised to find that Shane writes at an eighth-grade reading level. So does Joe. Ouch!

Then out of curiosity we decided to put some books by great writers through the reading-level calculator. The results were incredibly interesting.

We found that when you put Ernest Hemingway into a reading-level calculator, he gets a fourth-grade reading level. Put Cormac McCarthy, J. K. Rowling, and others who have sold millions and millions of books through calculator, and you'll discover that they all write at an extremely low reading level.

This got us obsessed. We put everything from our Kindles through the calculator. We made a bunch of charts. We looked at newspapers and magazines and their writers who are known for great, great writing.

The conclusion is simple, if initially counterintuitive: The most popular writers on a given topic write at lower reading levels on average than their peers. Writers who are able to take science and simplify it by several reading levels tend to be more successful than writers who write at a scientific level.

This is not only true of good sentence writing; it is our fourth element of fantastic storytelling. We call it *fluency*.

The principle is basically what one of Shane's favorite journalism teachers used to always say: "Great writing speeds you along."

She was right. A great story doesn't make you think about the words being used or the mechanics of the story itself. A great storyteller will speak at a level that doesn't force you to think about the vocabulary. You focus on what's going on, even if you don't know the definition of the occasional word. A great storyteller—whether in film, in writing, or in oral narration—grabs you with relatability, novelty, and tension. Then, they tell the story in a way that means you don't have to think about anything else.

Once again, *Star Wars* got this one right.

George Lucas always said that he wanted to have a sense of movement throughout his films. He didn't want people to have to slow down to think about what's going on.

Interestingly, *Star Wars'* mastery of this fluency wasn't really Lucas's doing at all. It was the work of his then-wife Marcia Lucas and the film's two other editors, Richard Chew and Paul Hirsch. They put the film together using fast cuts and quick transitions—a technique that few films had tried before. In science-fiction films before *Star Wars*, shots lasted longer and the action enfolded slower, with dramatic pauses abound. But *Star Wars* changed the game by moving the plot quickly, pulling the viewers through the journey. The three editors won an Academy Award for their work and helped make fast-cutting filmmaking incredibly popular.

Fluency, or the idea of a low reading level being better than a high reading level, or chopping a film up into hyperefficient shots, is a little bit counterintuitive. But the idea with story-telling is not to force people to use every bit of brainpower they have; it's to get them to focus on the characters, on the ten-sion, on relating to a theme, so that their brains can absorb the information.

This is where, once again, the 1990s prequel *Star Wars* films faltered.

They moved fast, yes. But they weren't fluent. They were confusing.

We recently rewatched all of the *Star Wars* films together with a friend who had never seen them. During the three pre-quels, she kept asking questions. Who's this? What's going on? She had to think about the plot. She didn't know who the hell Jar Jar Binks was, or why he talked like a Jamaican Gilbert Godfrey after inhaling a helium balloon. In the other films, she didn't have to ask questions every five minutes. She under-stood the story. She was completely engrossed.

Whether we're telling our story on Twitter, in a book or blog post, on a TV screen, or just at the bar with friends, it's incumbent on us to make each piece of our story flow to the next piece as efficiently as possible. We won't get compliments on how fluent our stories are—but that's the point. When you speak a language fluently, people only notice one thing: what you're saying.

3 Honing Your Storytelling Chops

B efore we get into the second half of this book, which is about how businesses (and businesspeople) can make use of storytelling in all sorts of ways, we're going to talk about a few timeless things that can help anyone get better at understanding and crafting great stories.

A lot of people we talk to in our line of work say, "Well, I'm no Hemingway." As we saw in the last section, neither are we!

And that's okay. We don't have to be Hemingway to be good at stories. Storytelling is part of what makes us human. If you have human DNA, you're built for story. Unfortunately, some of us give up on our storytelling ability too early.

In this chapter, we're going to help you see some patterns of great stories. Once you understand them, you're going to have an easier time noticing the good and bad stories in your life, and you may just have a hard time telling lame stories the next time you hit the bar with your coworkers.

Universal Storytelling Frameworks

See if you can guess what story this is.

We have a hero who starts in humble beginnings and answers the call of adventure. They leave home, get out of their comfort zone, receive training from a wise old mentor, and then go on a great journey. On this quest, they face a bad guy, almost lose everything, but eventually succeed and return home having changed.

What story are we talking about?

Is this *Star Wars*? *Harry Potter*? *The Hunger Games*? *The Odyssey*? *The Matrix*?

It's actually all of them.

This is a template for storytelling called the Hero's Journey. It comes from author Joseph Campbell, and it's everywhere. It's one of the most relatable storylines because it basically mirrors the journeys of our own lives. Understanding the Hero's Journey can give you insight into how to frame your own stories, whether it's the true story about your company or a fictional story that stirs your imagination.

The following diagram breaks down this Hero's Journey template, step by step.

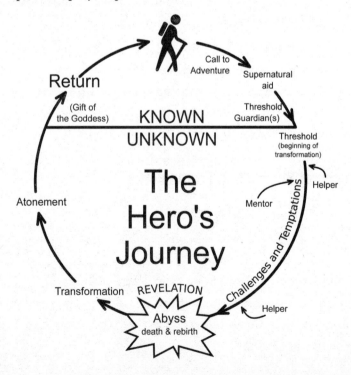

We start in an ordinary world. A humble character gets called to adventure and initially refuses but meets a wise mentor who trains them and convinces them to go on said adventure. They're then tested. They meet allies, and they make enemies. They approach a final battle and almost lose but, eventually, find it within themselves to succeed. They return home to an appropriate hero's welcome, transformed by the journey.

Let's walk through this from the lens of the greatest story ever told.

Yes, we're talking about *Star Wars* again. Let's step through a crude synopsis to see how well it matches Campbell's pattern:

In the first *Star Wars* film, we begin with the rather ordinary Luke Skywalker. He lives on a farm on a desert planet. One day he meets some robots who need help. They need to find a local hermit named Obi-Wan Kenobi. So Luke takes the robots to Obi-Wan, who basically says, "Luke, you need to go out and help save the universe." Luke initially says, "No, I have all this stuff going on," but Kenobi, who becomes Luke's mentor, convinces Luke that he should go. Kenobi trains him how to use a lightsaber, and Luke goes on an epic space adventure.

On the journey, Luke meets the villain, Darth Vader. He battles evil stormtroopers. He makes friends: Han Solo, Chewbacca, Princess Leia. And then he has to help defeat the superweapon, the Death Star. Nearly everything goes wrong, but in the end, Luke succeeds in blowing up the Death Star. The last scene of the movie is of Luke getting a metal put over his neck by the princess, who kisses him on the cheek. Now he is in his new home, a changed man, emboldened by the great power of the Force, which he can use on future adventures.

This is the Hero's Journey, which—modified in various ways—we see repeated in stories throughout history. The simple version of this is that pattern of tension that we learned from Aristotle. We have an ordinary person (what is), and we have adventure that lies ahead (what could be). The transference from one to the other is the journey.

In business, the case study is a rather common way marketers use this kind of story to sell a product or service. (Most of them are a little less entertaining stories than *Star Wars*, unfortunately.) A case study is the story of where a customer was, where they wanted to be—the tension!—and how they overcame that gap.

If you listen to podcasts, you'll hear this story told in most every ad. One of the most common ads is for Harry's razors, which tells the story of "Jeff and Andy, two ordinary guys who got fed up with paying way too much for razors at the pharmacy and decided to buy their own warehouse to sell affordable razors."

The problem with most brands' stories is they either don't fully utilize the four elements of great storytelling, or they don't walk us through enough of the steps of the Hero's Journey to capture our attention.

That's why these frameworks are so useful. They're a really easy way to ensure that we're more creative when we're coming up with stories or trying to convey information.

It's sort of like a haiku: If we told you right now to come up with a poem on the spot, you would probably have a tough time. But if we told you to come up with a haiku about *Star Wars*, you'd likely be able to do it. This framework helps you focus your creativity.

Another great story template comes from comedy writing. It starts similarly: A character is in a zone of comfort. But they want something, so they enter into an unfamiliar situation. They adapt, and eventually get what they're looking for but end up paying a heavy price for it. In the end, they return to their old situation having changed.

This is the plot of pretty much every episode of *Seinfeld*.

For example: During the sixth season of the show, George gets a toupee. This new situation is unfamiliar, but he likes it and quickly adapts to it. Once he has what he wants, though, he starts getting cocky. He goes on a date with a woman and behaves like a haughty jerk.

It turns out that his date, under her hat, is actually bald, too. When George is rude about this, she gets mad. His friends also get mad at him. "Do you see the irony here?" Elaine screams at him. "You're rejecting somebody because they're bald! You're bald!" She then grabs George's toupee and throws it out the window. A homeless man picks it up and puts it on.

The next day, George feels like himself again. "I tell you, when she threw that toupee out the window, it was the best thing that ever happened to me," he tells Jerry. "I feel like my old self again. Totally inadequate, completely insecure, para-noid, neurotic, it's a pleasure."

He also announces that he's going to keep seeing the bald woman. He returns to apologize to the woman, only for her to tell him that she only dates skinny guys.

So then George goes back home, having changed. He has his regular bald head now, but he's learned a lesson. (But because it's *Seinfeld*, he goes back to his old habits by the next episode.)

Both of these types of journeys are the journeys that we all go through in our lives, our businesses, and our families. As a storyteller, you can rely on these journey templates to shape your plots so you can fully unleash your creativity within.

The Ben Franklin Method for Improving Story Skills

When Benjamin Franklin was a boy, he yearned for a life at sea. This worried his father, so the two toured Boston, evaluating various eighteenth-century trades that didn't involve getting shipwrecked. Soon, young Ben found something he liked: books. Eagerly, Ben's father set his son up as an apprentice at a print shop.

Ben went on to become a revered statesman, a prolific inventor, and one of the most influential thinkers in American history. He owed most of that to his early years of voracious reading and meticulous writing—skills he honed while at the print shop.

Franklin wasn't born an academic savant. In fact, in his autobiography, he bemoans his subpar teenage writing skills and terrible math skills. To succeed at "letters," Franklin devised a system for mastering the writer's craft without the help of a tutor. To do so, he collected issues of the British culture and politics magazine, *The Spectator*, which contained some of the best writing of his day, and reverse engineered the prose.

He writes:

> I took some of the papers, and, making short hints of the
> sentiment in each sentence, laid them by a few days, and
> then, without looking at the book, try'd to compleat the
> papers again, by expressing each hinted sentiment at length,
> and as fully as it had been expressed before, in any suitable
> words that should come to hand.[1]

Basically, he took notes at a sentence level, sat on them for
a while, and tried to recreate the sentences from his own head,
without looking at the originals.

> Then I compared my Spectator with the original, discovered
> some of my faults, and corrected them. But I found I
> wanted a stock of words, or a readiness in recollecting and
> using them.[2]

Upon comparison, he found that his vocabulary was
lacking, and his prose was light on variety. So he tried the
same exercise, only instead of taking straightforward notes
on the articles he was imitating, he turned them into
poems.

> I took some of the tales and turned them into verse; and,
> after a time, when I had pretty well forgotten the prose,
> turned them back again.[3]

As his skill at imitating *Spectator*-style writing improved, he
upped the challenge:

> I also sometimes jumbled my collections of hints into con-
> fusion, and after some weeks endeavored to reduce them
> into the best order, before I began to form the full sentences
> and compleat the paper. This was to teach me method in
> the arrangement of thoughts.[4]

He did this over and over. Unlike the more passive method most writers use to improve their work (reading a lot), this exercise forced Franklin to pay attention to the tiny details that made the difference between decent writing and great writing:

> By comparing my work afterwards with the original, I discovered many faults and amended them; but I sometimes had the pleasure of fancying that, in certain particulars of small import, I had been lucky enough to improve the method or the language, and this encouraged me to think I might possibly in time come to be a tolerable English writer.[5]

When he says a "tolerable English writer," he's being humble. In a trivial amount of time, teenage Franklin became one of the best writers in New England and, shortly after that, a prodigious publisher.

Shane loves this story because he unwittingly did something very similar when he started training to become a journalist—and again when he embarked on writing his first book. He sat down and studied his favorite writers—Jon Ronson, Oscar Wilde, and J. K. Rowling. Rowling might seem like an odd addition here, but her work does something that is the hallmark of a great writing: It speeds you along. And instead of simply reading their work, he studied their sentences and made neurotic spreadsheets about them.

In his early days as a journalist, he studied the *New York Times* stories line by line: lengths, varieties, parts of speech, ledes, and kickers. He would sit down with a newspaper and a pad of paper and recreate the story by hand. When he started his best-selling book, *Smartcuts*—his first real work of significant length—he pulled out his favorite books and made spreadsheets of how the authors opened their chapters, set up tension between scenes, incorporated research and dialogue, used diction, and so on. He pulled apart his favorite feature stories by Gene Weingarten sentence by sentence, noting his use of adjectives (or lack thereof). Then, he would write sentences or paragraphs in different styles, trying to recreate the writing of his heroes. "How would Rowling write this paragraph?" "How would Gene write it?"

Through these exercises, he's gotten to the point where he's a tolerable enough English writer to make a career of doing what he loves.

But more importantly, just like Franklin, being a better writer and a student of good writing has helped him become a better student of everything. Good reading and writing ability helps you to be more persuasive, learn other disciplines, and apply critical feedback more effectively to any kind of work. When we're hiring for Contently, our first impression of a candidate is dramatically impacted by the clarity of their emails.

After building his writing muscles through his *Spectator* exercises, Franklin reported that he was finally able to teach himself mathematics:

> And now it was that, being on some occasion made asham'd of my ignorance in figures, which I had twice failed in learning when at school, I took Cocker's book of Arithmetick, and went through the whole by myself with great ease.[6]

Perhaps Ben's little secret for learning to write isn't so dissimilar from what MIT professor Seymour Papert's research has famously revealed: that children learn more effectively by building with LEGO bricks than they do by listening to lectures about architecture. It's not just the study of tiny details that accelerates learning; the act of assembling those details yourself makes a difference.

The Sludge Report

Shane had a professor at school who, every morning, would write a paragraph from someone's homework on the whiteboard for the whole class to see. More than half the time, it was from Shane's assignment.

The teacher called this the Sludge Report.

The challenge was to try to make the paragraph in question half as long, removing "sludge," or words and phrases that took longer than necessary to say something. This became the basis of our own self-editing process as writers. Every time we write, we look at each sentence and ask, "How could I make the point in fewer words?"

Whether you're writing for print or for the screen or just telling stories orally, periodically making your own Sludge Report will help you develop fluency.

Let's walk through a real example to show how it works. Below is a paragraph from a draft of an article from our blog at Contently. It's 46 words long:

> The disparity is likely a result of the fact that Twitter has become something of a media echo chamber. Even as Twitter has faded a bit compared to platforms like Facebook, Instagram, and Pinterest, it'll be interesting to see if the media can keep Twitter competitive.

Now the challenge. How can we make this half as long?

In the first sentence, we don't need "a result of the fact that." We can just say "because."

> The disparity is likely ~~a result of the fact that~~ because Twitter has become something of a media echo chamber. Even as Twitter has faded a bit compared to platforms like Facebook, Instagram, and Pinterest, it'll be interesting to see if the media can keep Twitter competitive.

Next: "Twitter has become something of a media echo chamber" doesn't need "something of." That makes the sentence weak anyway.

> The disparity is likely because Twitter has become ~~something of~~ a media echo chamber. Even as Twitter has faded a bit compared to platforms like Facebook, Instagram, and Pinterest, it'll be interesting to see if the media can keep Twitter competitive.

Now: "Even as Twitter has faded a bit." We don't need "a bit." It's faded.

> The disparity is likely because Twitter has become a media echo chamber. Even as Twitter has faded ~~a bit~~ compared to platforms like Facebook, Instagram, and Pinterest, it'll be interesting to see if the media can keep Twitter competitive.

Now: "platforms like Facebook, Instagram, and Pinterest."

We already know they're platforms, so we can take that out.

> The disparity is likely because Twitter has become a media echo chamber. Even as Twitter has faded compared to ~~platforms like~~ Facebook, Instagram, and Pinterest, it'll be interesting to see if the media can keep Twitter competitive.

"It'll be interesting to see if the media can keep Twitter competitive."

This one we could rephrase shorter: "It will be interesting to see how Twitter competes."

> The disparity is likely because Twitter has become a media echo chamber. Even as Twitter has faded compared to Facebook, Instagram, and Pinterest, it'll be interesting to see ~~if the media can keep~~ **how** Twitter **competes** ~~competitive~~.

Now we've changed this from 46 words to 29 words.

> The disparity is likely because Twitter has become a media echo chamber. Even as Twitter has faded compared to Facebook, Instagram, and Pinterest, it'll be interesting to see how Twitter competes.

What if we wanted to make it even shorter? Let's run the Sludge Report process again.

"The disparity is likely because Twitter has become a media echo chamber" is fine. But we can get rid of "Even as Twitter has faded compared to Facebook, Instagram, and Pinterest" and simply finish with "It'll be interesting to see how it competes against other platforms."

> The disparity is likely because Twitter has become a media echo chamber. It'll be interesting to see how it competes against other platforms.

We've now said the same thing as the original paragraph in half the words: 23.

You'll notice that we changed the word Twitter to "it." As Orwell said, "Why use a long word when you can use a short word?" Part of getting rid of sludge is using short words whenever possible.

You don't need to try to sound smart in your storytelling. As we said earlier, it's more important that your story is easy to understand and speeds the reader along.

Try it yourself. We dare you. The next time you're writing something, examine it paragraph by paragraph and ask, "How could I make this half as long?"

Using the Sludge method, you can improve the quality of anything you create and let your audience focus on what matters: the story.

4 Transforming Business with Storytelling

In 2008, General Electric's senior vice president of marketing (and soon to be chief marketing officer) Beth Comstock faced a big challenge. The global economy was tanking. The company's stock was plummeting. It had developed a reputation as stodgy and out-of-touch.

Comstock thought that this reputation was crazy. GE made some of the most exciting inventions in the world, from jet engines to solar generators. It had a unique, startup-esque culture—rare for a Fortune 500 company. This was part of its commitment to maintaining the spirit of invention that Thomas Edison had infused in the company 130 years prior. But no one outside of GE really knew about that. Comstock realized that needed to change.

But how? The answer, she realized, was that they had to do a better job of telling their story.

For the previous 28 months, Comstock had been running digital marketing for NBC Universal, the company responsible behind hits like *Jurassic Park* and *30 Rock*. Perhaps taking a page from NBCU's book could help turn GE's reputation around, Comstock thought. Instead of thinking like a marketer, GE could solve its problem by thinking like a media company. Like a storyteller.

Comstock and her team got to work. They launched a blog called *GE Reports*, which documented the stories behind the company's innovations around the world—everything from brain scanners to high-speed trains. They partnered with artists to make EDM songs out of jet engine sounds, and filmed pop-sci documentaries about classic GE inventions. Comstock's team made sure GE was the first big brand to create content on pretty much every new social channel that emerged—from Pinterest to Periscope. They made six-second videos of science experiments and hilarious listicles about gravity.

With Comstock's guidance, storytelling became a force that changed the company's reputation, both internally and externally. It put GE innovation on display and invited share-holders and customers to reimagine the company as a cutting-edge tech company, rather than an old-school power company. And this played a central role in the company's remarkable postrecession turnaround.

Making this happen inside a massive company like GE is no easy feat. Just getting a Facebook post approved can take 27 lawyers and a fax machine inside some big companies. So how did GE do it?

If your experience is the same as ours, you know that the default mode at large companies is to play it safe. This isn't because of a lack of creativity. It's because creativity is, by nature, risky. Why try something new when it might cost you your job? But here's the thing: If great stories require novelty, like we've learned, then they inherently require us to step out-side of our comfort zone. We have to take risks without fearing for our jobs.

At a time when great vanguards of great science storytell-ing—newspapers and magazines—were collapsing and cutting staff, Comstock gave GE's story laboratory the resources and freedom to fill a creative void. In fact, when you talk to anyone who's worked with her, that's the first thing they'll tell you.

"There's a freedom to experiment and a tolerance to fail," Linda Boff, Comstock's protégé and the current CMO of GE, told us. "Beth has more than tolerance. She's such an innovator and really supports us. As she told us, she's obsessed with one question: "How do we keep the company fresh? How do we make sure that we stay relevant and contemporary, and we're meaningful to new audiences?"[1]

That vision wasn't just felt in the executive board room. It was communicated down the chain to the storytellers themselves. Just listen to Melissa Lafsky Wall, a veteran editor and content strategist who helped launch *GE Reports*:

"Beth had vision. GE had vision. It felt like an exciting place to be. Everywhere I had been working felt like death—'This magazine is going to close,' 'We're working hard but there's no future here'—but this felt like an opportunity where an organization was excited about creating content. And that created a sense of possibility, a sense of freedom."[2]

The point here isn't just that Beth Comstock is amazing and that anyone who wants to reinvent their business through great content should hire her. (Although they probably should.) It's that her approach was dead on.

She had a vision, and used storytelling to achieve it, creative risks be damned.

What GE did is rare. At a crucial point for the company, the industrial giant invested in telling bold stories, and it's not a coincidence that years of wild success followed.

GE had the rare combination that makes for great brand storytellers: a culture of storytelling that plans for success but isn't afraid of failure. As a result, content has touched every

part of their business. GE's content has increased job applications by 800 percent, made the company a favorite of science
nerds on Reddit, and helped more than quadruple its stock,
from $7.06 in March 2009 to $31.44 at the time of this
writing. Millions of people read their articles and watch their
videos every month. They share them with their friends and
coworkers. They're eager advocates for GE.

Now that we've covered the fundamentals of great storytelling, for the rest of the book we're going to discuss the art
and science of leveraging it for your organization—the art of
harnessing your creativity, and the science of taking a data-
driven approach to developing a content strategy and planning
for success.

In other words, we're going to show you how to do the
kinds of things that great storytelling companies like GE do.
We're going to demonstrate how to use storytelling to make
every part of a business better.

To start, let's travel back to 1940s' New York for the story
of a mayor who did something that makes Michael Bloomberg's soda ban look like amateur hour.

How Stories Make Products and Services Better

In 1942, Fiorello La Guardia, the mayor of New York, organized a sudden citywide raid. All at once, he sent his police
officers throughout the boroughs. They busted into bars,
lounges, gambling parlors, and clubs to confiscate some specific items that La Guardia was after.

And then the mayor ceremoniously destroyed these items.
With a sledgehammer.

What was this contraband that Mayor La Guardia hated so much that he not only banned it, but personally smashed it? Was it drug manufacturing equipment? Weapons? Anti–La Guardia propaganda?

Nope. They were pinball machines.

Mayor La Guardia's smash fest was, in fact, part of a great pinball machine ban that swept America. Chicago, San Francisco, and other major cities also went after the games. For decades, pinball all but completely disappeared.

But why did La Guardia and other mayors hate pinball? Why did such an innocent game get targeted, and not, say, Risk, the game of maniacal global domination?

It was because of a story about pinball.

The story was that pinball machine owners were hustling children for their lunch money. Because the game was exciting and flashy, it attracted kids. And the game was addicting. Furthermore, the story went, pinball was almost purely a game of chance, not something a kid could get good at. So kids were being sucked in and getting ripped off. Rumor had it, they were so addicted they weren't even eating.

It didn't matter that this story wasn't really true. It turned pinball into something that a politician could use to make a point and look good.

"I'm on the side of your kids," someone like La Guardia might say, while smashing a pinball machine with a sledgehammer. Trading the votes of a few pinball machine owners for those of a lot of paranoid parents was an effective strategy.

In other words, a story about a product destroyed the product.

That's not the end of pinball's story, but before we get back to it, let's look at another story about another machine: The magnetic resonance imaging machine, or MRI.

A few years ago, General Electric assigned Doug Dietz, one of its top product designers, to bring its MRI machine into the twenty-first century.

These lifesaving machines are big, bulky, and expensive contraptions that help doctors see inside someone's body. GE spent tens of millions of dollars on the redesign. Dietz turned the old, boxy machine into a sleek, donut-shaped device that looked like it belonged on a spaceship. It was energy efficient and more advanced than anything on the market.

As the company started rolling out the improved machines, Dietz visited a hospital to see how patients were responding to the new design.

What he saw made him want to cry.

He saw the doctors take a tiny child into the MRI room. Meanwhile, the kid was in tears. "Mommy, mommy, please don't make me go into the machine again."

Dietz realized something that hadn't occurred to him during the design process. To a little kid, an MRI machine is terrifying. You walk into a bright-lit room where strangers strap you to a board and slide you inside a hole for half an hour—all by yourself. There's a needle in your arm, loud clanking noises, and dire warnings about how you need to hold still or they'll have to do it all over again.

GE's new MRI, though beautiful and energy efficient, was no exception. It was a scary experience.

Dietz was crestfallen. He realized that some of the patients who he cared about the most—the vulnerable, sick kids who his machine might help save—hated his creation. Would he have to go back to the drawing board to make a new one that wasn't so terrifying?

As Dietz considered the millions of dollars another redesign might cost, he was struck with an idea.

What if instead of making a completely new machine, they turned the current machine into an adventure?

What if the night before a little girl went in for an MRI, her parents read her a storybook about the pirate adventure she would go on in the morning? In the book, she'd meet Marcela the Monkey and Tina the Toucan, and all of her new friends who'd be waiting at the hospital. And then when she went to the hospital the next day, what if the doctors and nurses were dressed as characters from the book? The adventure from the book would continue in a role-play in the hospital, culminating in the part where she had to get on the lifeboat to drift past one of the pirate ships and get to her friends.

This part would, of course, be the actual MRI scan. But the child would experience the scan as part of a story, while staring at pictures of her pirate adventure friends on the ceiling of the scanner. And she'd have a really good reason to lay still—so the pirates don't catch us!

It turns out that painting an MRI machine to look like a pirate ship is a lot cheaper than designing a whole new one. The GE team trained doctors and nurses on their pirate adventure plan and turned the MRI experience from a terrible ordeal into a riveting adventure.

And the most wonderful part is this: Kids went from saying, "Mommy, please don't let me go into the scary machine
again!" to "Can I go again?"

So far in this book we've talked a lot about how stories
help people connect to each other and to businesses. These
two stories illustrate how stories can also help us change our
minds about products. In one case, a story about a product
ruined it. In another case, a story about a product saved it.

Stories have a huge impact on the way people decide
what products to buy. Scores of studies show that today's
consumers are more likely to do business with companies
that develop their products thoughtfully and ethically. Most
middle-class consumers would rather buy something with a
positive or interesting backstory, even if it's a little more
expensive. We like to know when our coffee is harvested by
families in Ecuador who care about the environment and are
paid fairly. We'll pay more for the basketball shoes that
Lebron James codesigned than ones created by some anon-
ymous designer.

For instance, Shane was recently in the market for a nice
watch. He'd never owned a watch that cost more than $20, so
for his birthday, he decided to splurge and buy himself one for
a few hundred. When he started looking, he remembered a
brand called Shinola whose story he had heard a few times.

Shinola was founded in Detroit when the city was having a
really hard time. Thousands of manufacturing jobs were moving overseas. Wealthy and middle-class residents were moving
out, turning parts of the city into ghost towns. Crime was
high, buildings were abandoned, and infrastructure was
crumbling.

Shinola's mission was to bring manufacturing jobs back to Detroit by retraining bereaved auto workers and factory employees to make bicycles and watches. They wanted to make solid, quality, American products that were worth paying more for, and that put food on the table for hard-working Detroit citizens.

Remembering this story, he checked out Shinola's watches. They were awesome. Substantial, and a beautiful product. And bonus: Buying one would make him a small part of the story of Detroit's revival that Shinola was telling.

So he bought one, and he loved it so much that he bought a matching one for his best friend's birthday. (So cute, we know.) Then when Shinola started manufacturing turntables, he bought one of those, too.

Shinola's products are great, but their story is what got him to try them in the first place.

And this brings us back to pinball.

After three decades without pinball, the game suddenly roared back to life in the 1970s, 1980s, and early 1990s. The reason? *Star Wars.*

We're only half-kidding. While America lined up for *Jaws* and *Star Wars* and *Indiana Jones*, pinball machine makers came up with an idea: Why not incorporate these popular stories into pinball games themselves? The games started featuring artwork from popular movies and TV shows and musical acts. You played as your favorite characters or you played to fight or rescue them.

Suddenly pinball machines were everywhere. Geeky kids proved to the world—on camera—that pinball could be more than a game of chance, and the political campaign against them evaporated. Movie buffs soon lined up to relive their favorite films in pinball form, and the pinball industry boomed. (Fun fact, the best-selling pinball game of all time was created during this era: The Addams Family.) By incorporating stories into the product, pinball makers gave consumers a lot of reasons to play pinball, even though it was always pretty much the same game.

We'll do a lot because of a good story. We'll support destroying a product associated with a bad story. We'll change our minds about a product if it incorporates a good story. We'll pay a little extra for a product that has an inspirational backstory. And we'll give something a second chance because of a redemption story.

We might even get excited about a day full of TV commercials if the stories are good.

Stories Make Advertising Better

A few years ago, researchers at Johns Hopkins University examined Super Bowl ads to see who was getting the best bang for their buck. As of the time of this writing, a Super Bowl ad on CBS cost $166,666 per second. That's $10 million per minute.

The Super Bowl is one of the few occasions where TV audiences are actually happy to watch the commercials. Because the ads are so expensive, advertisers put a lot of effort into making them great. So whereas we skip commercials during the rest of the year, we'll run back from the kitchen with a mouthful of potato chips to catch Super Bowl commercials.

Of course, not all of the Super Bowl ads are great. The Hopkins researchers wanted to know what made the biggest difference between a Super Bowl ad people loved and one they didn't.

They took several years of Super Bowl ads and catalogued them by various factors: humor, length, sexiness, subject matter, use of cute animals, and other elements. Then they looked at which ads were the most popular to see which of these factors mattered the most.

What they found was surprising. It turns out that neither jokes nor cute animals nor sexy ladies made a Super Bowl ad popular.

The best ads were the ones that had strong narrative arcs.

In other words, the best ads were great stories.

But let's not underestimate the cute animals, since they play a big part in our favorite story about just how much storytelling is upending advertising.

In 2014, BuzzFeed was in the midst of launching a new kind of advertising agency. Two years earlier, they had hired Ze Frank—one of the Internet's most successful early video creators—to launch BuzzFeed Motion Pictures, a studio that would create original video for the digital media startup and its advertisers.

Most advertising videos shops follow an age-old model: They sell a flashy idea for an ad spot to a client, invest a huge budget to produce the spot, and buy media to support it. The entire exercise is an educated act of faith.

BuzzFeed and Frank, however, wanted to do things differently. Since its beginnings in November 2006, BuzzFeed's founder Jonah Peretti had been obsessed with the science of how content spreads online. BuzzFeed constantly tinkered with how they created and distributed content, making slight adjustments to headlines, story structure, and content strategy. This allowed them to skyrocket to more than 150 million readers, surpassing the digital reach of major legacy publishers like the *New York Times*.

BuzzFeed never ran banner ads. Rather, it created content on behalf of advertisers and doubled down on original videos as their primary advertising offering.

So when Purina came to BuzzFeed in 2014 to run an advertising campaign, Frank didn't pitch them on a big spot. Instead, Frank proposed to create a series of short videos. The two companies agreed to make a set number of videos and test to see which one resonated with BuzzFeed's audience. The idea was to test a bunch of different storytelling approaches against a broader theme until they found a hit, just like Buzz-Feed had always done with their regular (nonadvertiser) stories.

In a *Fast Company* profile, former BuzzFeed CMO Greg Cooper recalled showing a two-minute comic video story they created to a Purina executive. The exec audibly gasped when he saw it, surprised by how different the video was from a traditional ad spot.

The video showed an older cat schooling a new kitten in the ways of the world, explaining the strange behavior of their humans and the best spots in the apartment to hang out. ("On special occasions, they will leave the underwear drawer open to signal their appreciation . . . of me," the older cat tells the kitten. "To be clear it's my spot. It's perfect in there. It's like sleeping in underwear. Well . . . that's exactly what it is.")

The video, entitled *Dear Kitten*, would become the most famous piece of social advertising to date, generating more than 27 million views on YouTube. (Its sequels have racked up more than 40 million additional views.) But the most interesting thing about is how it was developed: through a rigorous series of trial and error tests. The first four videos BuzzFeed made for Purina flopped. It took a half-dozen videos before they developed a hit.

"It sounds like a revolution," Cooper told us. "Large corporations don't like revolutions. They like predictability. They like incremental growth."[3]

But those corporations are quickly changing their tune. They're realizing that the most effective way to find a hit is to strategically create content, test how it'll connect with audiences, and then optimize the approach based on what they learned. We'll get to more on that in a bit!

Stories Make Your Sales Conversions Better

The fastest-growing business in the history of the world did something clever to beat its competition. It got people to open emails and buy products at an outrageous rate—through stories.

The company was called Groupon. Launched in Chicago in 2008, Groupon sent a daily email that told you about a great deal at a local business near you. Before long, a lot of other companies started offering daily deals similar to Groupon. Soon the company had two kinds of competitors: daily deal sites and every other email in your inbox that might get in the way of you clicking on Groupon's offer.

So Groupon hired writers from Second City, the renowned comedy school, to punch up its emails. They wrote hilarious, fictional backstories behind every product and service Groupon offered.

This led to two things: First, people started opening the emails just to read the funny stories. This led to an exceptionally high email open rate, and a big boost in sales. Even if people didn't want to buy a coupon, they might, say, send a hilarious Groupon for laser hair removal to a particularly hairy friend.

Groupon ended up having a lot of business problems because it grew so fast, but the moral of its story is something that any business can learn from: Great stories—whether funny or fictional or true—can dramatically improve sales.

One of our favorite examples of a company using stories to increase sales conversion rate is Zady. It sells what it calls "sustainable fashion," or apparel sourced ethically, in an environmentally friendly way.

When you browse Zady.com and click on a pair of indigo skinny jeans, you don't just find the price and pictures. You also get the story of the cute couple in Kentucky that makes the jeans in their garage. You learn about their dog, the story of how they met, and the love and care they put into making those jeans.

These stories increase Zady's conversion rate—the percentage of people who buy a product when they land on the product page. But they also stick in your mind, so the next time you're in the market for indigo skinny jeans, you're probably going to remember that story. That means there's a good chance that you'll go back to Zady to buy those jeans, rather than buying Levi's at the department store.

But one of the interesting things about stories is that they don't just help you sell products. They also help you sell your company to prospective employees.

Stories Make Your Hiring Process Better

If you watch a lot of primetime TV, there's a good chance you've met Owen.

Owen is the fictional engineer and star of GE's cleverly self-deprecating commercials that have run over the past couple years. The spots follow Owen as he tries to explain his new cool new job developing breakthrough code as a GE engineer to his befuddled friends and family, who think that he's going to go work on a train or in a warehouse.

Owen sparked one of the most successful recruiting campaigns in GE's history. Applications for engineering positions at GE went up by 800 percent. 800 percent! That's crucial for a company that's trying to win a talent war with Facebook, Snapchat, Google, and every other sexy startup in Silicon Valley.

And yet, it wasn't supposed to be a recruiting campaign at all.

According to Linda Boff, the GE CMO we met earlier, they didn't even think of the commercials as a recruiting campaign when they made them. They just wanted to find an interesting and self-deprecating way to let people know that, yes, GE is a really cool company.

And not only did the videos attract tons of new people applying to work at GE, they also gave the company a big morale boost.

"People inside the company are just in love with the campaign," Boff told us.[4]

Boff even brought the actor who played Owen to some of GE's internal events. The reaction, among GE employees, was like they'd brought the Beatles back together. That's because while Owen was a story about GE, it was also a story about the people who worked there.

The campaign showed that there are no real boundaries between internal and external marketing anymore. When you tell a great story that inspires the outside world, it also inspires the people inside your four walls.

Stories Build Your Brand

In July 2016, Unilever shocked the business world. They were purchasing Dollar Shave Club—a startup dreamed up just five years earlier by an improv comedian named Michael Dubin—for $1 billion.

Reporters were baffled. Similar e-commerce subscription startups like Birchbox, Trunk Club, and Stitch Fix had failed to attract anywhere near the same interest. Plus, Dollar Shave Club sold blades that paled in comparison to the high-tech razors that brands Gillette and Schick were famous for. Heck, it didn't even make its own razors! It just bought them wholesale from manufacturers in China and resold them. The billion-dollar price tag was also five times Dollar Shave Club's expected 2016 revenue—a near-unprecedented multiple for a retail startup.

So why did Unilever pay such an unprecedented price tag? As forward-thinking analysts began to explain, it wasn't about revenue. It was about the company's relationships—with customers, and consumers at large. Relationships that began with possibly the greatest startup launch video of all time.

In 1990, a group of comedians that included Amy Poehler, Adam McKay, Ian Roberts, and Horatio Sanz had created an improv group called The Upright Citizen's Brigade (UCB). Before long, the UCB had its own Comedy Central TV show and served as a talent pipeline to *Saturday Night Live*. As class offerings expanded, it became the destination for the thousands of young creatives who stumbled out of their college acting classes and into the bright lights of New York City each year.

In the early 2000s, Dollar Shave Club founder Michael Dubin was one of those young creatives. For eight years, he honed his craft at UCB while working in various television and marketing jobs. In December 2010, he found himself at a Christmas party talking to one of his father's friends. The conversation took an unexpected turn, and before long, the family friend was asking him for help selling 250,000 razors he had acquired from Asia. (We've all been there, right?) The conversation would have weirded a lot of people out, but it gave Dubin an idea. What if he started a service that would eliminate the expense and hassle of selling razor blades? What if they just showed up at your door each month for $1 each?

Faced with the challenge of getting the startup off the ground and attracting investors, Dubin knew that he had to speak to men like him. Men who were fed up with a razor monopoly that forced them to pay more than $20 for just a few blades. And so he bet big on what he does best. He created a hilarious video to connect with his target audience and cast him as the protagonist in the Hero's Journey of his own brand.

If you're one of the few earthlings who managed to avoid seeing it, go watch it now here: http://sha.ne/storiesdsc.

"Are our blades any good?" Dubin asks in the beginning of the video. "No, our blades are fucking great."

What follows is 90 seconds of absolute absurdity that nonetheless touts all of the features of Dollar Shave Club's razors. There's a toddler shaving a man's head, polio jokes, a machete, a clumsy bear, a giant American flag, and perhaps the best "make it rain" scene of all time.

The rough cut of the video convinced former Myspace CEO Michael Jones to sign on as Dubin's partner. When the video was released on March 6, 2012, it went viral. The startup got more than 12,000 orders in the first 48 hours.

Dollar Shave Club's origin story highlights something powerful: The economics of marketing are changing quickly, with great content as the ultimate currency. As a result, brands that embrace great storytelling can achieve an incredible advantage over their competition.

As we noted previously in this book, the principles behind Dubin's success aren't new. Companies have always told stories to drive sales. From the very first barters made to the present day, that hasn't changed. But everything else has.

The sheer pace of technological change in how we are able to communicate our stories to each other—from the birth of radio a century ago to the hurricane of social media apps that's marked the 2010s—can be daunting for brands.

On one hand, it presents a huge opportunity. Content is being published everywhere, and consumers are now immersed in stories everywhere they go. Per comScore, time spent with digital media tripled between 2010 and 2016. At last count, 65 percent of all time spent with digital media occurred on mobile devices, consumed primarily via social networks. As a result, companies that excel at storytelling can reach their target customers more effectively and at greater scale than traditional advertising ever offered—all at a fraction of the cost.

On the other hand, there's more content now than ever. At a conference in 2010, Google CEO Eric Schmidt revealed that we create as much information every two days as we did in human history up until 2003, a figure that's only increased since.

As a result, brands can't create mediocre content and expect to stand out. Half-baked content simply has little chance of breaking through on social or search.

"There's not a whole lot of value in writing a decent blog post anymore. [There's not a lot of value] unless you can be pretty extraordinary," SEO and content analyst Rand Fishkin, who also founded Moz, told us. "Ask: If they're searching for an answer to a question, would they rather reach your piece of content than anything else on the Internet right now? Unless the answer is a slam dunk, 'Yes, this is 10 times better than anything else out there,' I'm not necessarily sure it's worth publishing."[5]

But when you do create something amazing that stands out? The results are staggering.

Dubin and Dollar Shave Club continued to crank out hilarious videos that their target audience watched millions of times and shared enthusiastically. One of the best follow-ups, "Let's Talk about #2," introduced their new butt wipes product and made more jokes about bears pooping than you ever thought you'd see in a brand video.

It also started shipping *The Bathroom Minutes*, a small comic newspaper, with every order. And in late 2015, it launched MEL, one of the most ambitious editorial sites ever launched by a brand.

As Contently managing editor Jordan Teicher wrote in *The Content Strategist*: "MEL is a great example of how ambitious storytelling can stand out if brands stop trying to play it safe. It's the only place you can read articles like 'I Went Shark Fishing and Accidentally Caught a Kilo of Coke' or watch short documentaries about subjects like former Harvard graduates who become medieval fighters."[6]

In total, these videos helped build an incredibly strong brand and lasting relationships with consumers. Moreover, they helped Dollar Shave Club achieve a financial exit that seemed impossible just a few years before.

"There are two things that drive multiples: the financial metrics and the story," David Pakman, a partner at Venrock and an early investor in Dollar Shave Club, told Bloomberg.[7]

So how do you find a way for your brand to tell billion-dollar stories? The story of how we did it at Contently is a good segue into the content strategy formula that makes up the next two chapters of this book.

How We Built the Most Influential Content Strategy Blog on Earth

When Joe first started running our blog *The Content Strategist*, we only had about 14,000 monthly readers and a couple thousand newsletter subscribers. Shane had been blogging haphazardly with our buddy Sam and some freelancers while building the business and finally decided we needed a full-time editor to push the pedal and hold the steering wheel.

As a trade publication, we weren't going to turn into BuzzFeed, but given the booming interest in content marketing, there was clearly an opportunity in front of us to grab the attention of a niche audience. Three years after Joe took over, half a million marketers and media folks read our blog on a given month, and our newsletter had eclipsed 100,000 devoted subscribers. Our stories were generating thousands of high-quality leads for our software business each month, and thus paying its cost of production off tenfold. And we'd won numerous accolades, including Best Brand Publication at the 2016 Digiday Awards.

Here's how we did it:

#1: Committing to a Mission

You've probably heard the tired cliché that content marketing, the overarching practice of using stories to boost your brand, is "a marathon and not a sprint." Someone says this at damn near every marketing conference. But it's actually a pretty crappy metaphor.

In reality, content marketing is more like a political campaign. You have to introduce yourself to people and earn their trust. You have to listen to their concerns. You can't just begin your campaign by brazenly demanding that people give you support before you do anything to earn it. More than anything, you need a mission that drives your content and resonates with people.

At Contently, we talk extensively about how we want to "build a better media world." This may sound like a corporate platitude, but it's not. It's our mission.

From the onset, we knew this mantra would drive *The Content Strategist*. We believed we could make the media world better by helping brands work with great tools and talented creatives to tell stories that people actually want to engage with. For us, storytelling was the Force. And all of those crappy "LOOK AT ME!" ads that stalked people around the Internet and got in the way of what they actually were trying to do online? To us, that was the dark side.

When we first started, our job was to show marketers the light side by reporting on the good and the bad in the content marketing industry and by publishing helpful strategy tips, analysis, and advice. We needed to have editorial integrity and prioritize honesty and transparency over company messaging. If we wanted to help people, we had to gain their trust, and we weren't going to do that by pushing Contently's software every third paragraph.

We were lucky enough to work at a company founded and staffed by journalists who trusted us to do that. It quickly started to pay off. Within six months, we grew from 14,000 to 100,000 readers.

This isn't a revolutionary tactic. Every successful content marketing example (GE, Casper, Red Bull, Dollar Shave Club,

Moz, Marriott, etc.) has followed a similar audience-first ethos. They're guided by a mission to do right by the people they want to build relationships with.

#2: Getting Smart about Audience

By the fall of 2014, the business side of Contently was pretty pleased with our editorial operation. Our traffic growth was driving more leads and opportunities. And as a result, our CEO Joe decided to give our editorial team more budget.

We launched a sister site called The Freelancer to expand our editorial mission to the creative community. A young freelancer for the *Wall Street Journal*, Jordan Teicher, became our second full-time editor. Our former editorial intern, Kieran Dahl, became our social media editor. And in many ways, he's the star of this second phase.

Having been handed a bigger budget due to our success so far, we gave Kieran a small chunk of change to experiment with using paid Facebook ads to reach more people with our stories, a tactic that was becoming incredibly popular among publishers. We had no interest in juicing pageviews (after all, we weren't selling ads), but we did want to use Contently Analytics to see if we could increase meaningful engagement, drive conversions, and acquire loyal readers who might not have known about *The Content Strategist*.

Essentially, we used our analytics to understand which stories we could promote on Facebook and get unusually high returns. A cheap cost per click (CPC) is great, but you really want stories that will cause readers to do things like:

- Spend a lot of time with your content
- Finish the majority of the story they land on
- Read other content afterward
- Share the story on their social networks
- Become email subscribers
- Download premium content
- Visit product pages and fill out demo request forms

Take, for example, an interview that Joe did with Seth Godin. People love Seth Godin, so it was superpopular. Not only did tons of people click on it, but they spent five minutes reading it on average—125 percent better than our average story. And when we promoted it on Facebook, it had a cheap CPC. Plus, it caused lots of people to subscribe to our newsletter and become loyal readers. So it just made sense for us to keep promoting it. After all, if you're spending $500 to produce a piece of content, it often makes sense to spend an extra $50 to get twice the returns.

Promoting stories like this helped us quickly convert readers coming from Facebook into newsletter subscribers—who are by far the people most likely to be loyal readers of your site. Over the next six months, our audience grew to more than 200,000 readers.

#3: Establishing a Strategic Methodology

When you're running a publication, there's a pretty strong temptation to go with your gut.

This isn't always a bad thing. As an editor, you often need to trust yourself and jump on a story, especially when it's a popular topic and the opportunity cost of sitting on your hands is high.

But you also need to regularly step back and evaluate what's working. One of the most important tactics is to tag your story (by topic, persona, format, and other details), and compare production metrics to performance metrics. That way you can see which stories are under- or overperforming against your goals on a per-story basis.

This allows you to easily see what topics and formats you're relying on too much and which ones you're not using enough.

We also then examine what content performs best across different channels and tailor our distribution strategy accordingly. This ensures that we're spending our time and money wisely—and getting the right content to the right people.

When we started doing this religiously, we saw a lot of blind spots and missed opportunities. For instance, "fun content"—like quizzes, comics, and humor pieces—was actually one of the most effective ways for us to attract loyal readers. On the flip side, straight industry news pieces (without in-depth analysis) tended to underperform. And while a piece on a subject like measuring ROI or conducting a content audit might not attract as many readers as a fun quiz, it was very effective at engaging prospects already interested in purchasing Contently's software. Nowadays, we do a deep dive every month. But we recommend that you go through this kind of review at least every three months. For us, it did wonders, allowing us to nearly double our audience yet again. And we've seen our clients do the same.

Although our tactics have become more sophisticated—and they'll certainly change as the Internet changes—the underlying philosophy remains the same: We want to serve our audience. We want to tell the most interesting and useful stories about content marketing and the tech industry so that our audience remembers what they've learned and succeeds at their job. If there's a secret to brand storytelling, it's just that.

5 The Killer Formula for Building an Audience

In this book, we've covered how great stories build relationships and make people care. And that the businesses that historically have had the best relationships with their customers are the ones where storytelling is their business. We're talking about newspapers. Magazines. Television networks. Netflix. HBO. These are businesses that have the loyal subscribers the rest of us have had to pay money to reach.

So what can we learn from them? What's their secret? If you look closely, you'll notice that all of them essentially follow the same time-tested playbook.

The CCO Pattern: Create, Connect, Optimize

Throughout history, there's a pattern for how media organizations have used storytelling to build audiences. The pattern starts with the very first example of mass media in history, during the Italian Renaissance.

Sixteenth-century Europe was home to a flurry of art, commerce, and science. Wealthy families began gaining power, and wars and skirmishes were frequent.

This meant there was also a lot of gossip.

The very first mass media business was the gossip rag. Think of it as an ancient TMZ. Every day, gossip writers would run around cities like Milan to gather the news and rumors of the day. They'd go to the churches, markets, and barracks to find scuttlebutt. Then they'd converge at a writing house and create a newsletter with all the rumors fit to linotype.

They would print all that gossip using the fanciest new technology: the recently invented printing press. And then they would hand out the newsletters, called *Avvisi*, around town.

The *Avvisi* writers learned a few things very quickly. First, while the printing press was the latest and greatest tech, it was cumbersome to operate. Some clever writers realized that if they hand-copied their *Avvisi*, they could beat their peers to market.

Turns out, the public was more interested in timely gossip than fancy printed fonts. So, the handwritten *Avvisi* became more popular. Soon enough, all of the *Avvisi* writers stopped using the printing press entirely.

The second thing the gossip writers learned was that, if you wrote something that angered someone in power, you might get your head chopped off. This didn't have to happen very many times for the surviving *Avvisi* writers to stop putting their names on their newsletters. They began hiding their identities and writing in secret. To avoid blowing their cover, they adjusted their distribution strategy by posting the *Avvisi* in public places at night.

With these modifications, the people got what they wanted (news about Leonardo's latest crush, ASAP), and the Avvisi writers got what they wanted (their heads, intact).

We learn a few things from this story. First, it pays to figure out what the audience wants before you decide what technology to use. Most of us do this backward. We get so excited about the latest SnapGoggle Pokeball Platform that we often forget that people want good stories.

The second thing we learn is that good audience-building strategy follows a pattern.

CREATE

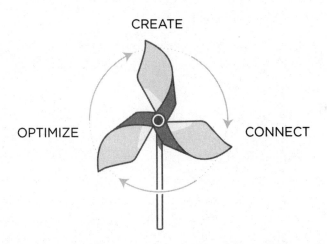

OPTIMIZE   CONNECT

At Contently, we call this the *flywheel*. First, you create content, you figure out how to get it to people, and then you optimize both what you create and how you deliver it.

Our *Avvisi* writers printed up the gossip (create), handed it around town (connect), and then figured out that people wanted the gossip faster (optimize).

So they copied by hand (create), handed it out around town (connect), and then figured out they were liable to get their heads chopped off (optimize).

So *then* they wrote anonymously (create), posted the *Avvisi* in public places at night (connect), and kept their heads (optimize).

And thus, a new industry of media moguls with fully-intact heads was born!

Fast-forward 200 years to the newspaper wars of the 1800s, and the same pattern played out again.

By this time, printing press technology had become more efficient than copying by hand.

In the mid-nineteenth century in big cities like New York, anyone wealthy enough to afford a printing press seemed to be launching a newspaper.

The strategy of all the newspapers was basically the same: News reporters would run around town gathering stories. They would dictate their notes to writers (or write the stories themselves), and each day they'd print out a fresh paper with yesterday's news. Then a bunch of chain-smoking newsboys, dressed like modern Brooklyn hipsters, would stand on street corners and shout the headlines. The goal was to catch the attention of commuters as they walked to work. If a headline interested you, you'd pay the newsboy a penny for a paper.

Newspaper owners discovered a few problems with this strategy. First, there were too many papers using this same strategy—and a glut of content as a result. Newspapers started to become commodities, and people didn't much differentiate between papers.

This led to a loyalty problem. Newspaper owners such as Joseph Pulitzer of *New York World* and William Randolph Hearst of the *New York Journal* wanted market share. But few people seemed to say, things like "I'm a *New York World* gal" or "I only read the *Journal*."

This also led to a quality problem. If you made sales through attention-grabbing headlines, that meant you needed really juicy headlines all the time. Suddenly, every headline was dark and sensational. "Mad Woman Leaps from Bridge!" "War Is Coming!" These stories got the attention of commuters but were often disingenuous.

Newspapers not only didn't win loyalty this way, but they also started to have a trust problem. (Does any of this sound familiar in the Facebook era?)

This led to yet another issue. Newspapers were happy for people to buy copies on the street, but what they really wanted were subscribers. They wanted people to pay a monthly fee to have the newsboys deliver the news to their door. This was a much more attractive business model, but it required the kind of loyalty the papers didn't have.

That all changed when Pulitzer hired an ambitious young woman named Nellie Bly, who assertively walked in one day asking for a job widely considered unsuitable for a woman at the time. She's one of our favorite people in history, and one of the first game-changing journalists in America.

While other reporters chased headlines about crazy people jumping from bridges, Bly decided to investigate New York's mental health system. She pretended to be crazy so she could get locked up in an asylum.

Bly spent 10 days in the asylum before Pulitzer got her out. She then wrote a multipart series for the *New York World* about the experience.

The story exploded. New Yorkers were hungry for each new installment. The series detailed the horrible conditions for patients, the ghastly behavior of the doctors and nurses, and the many cracks in the mental health system.

New York City, and soon the rest of America, began reforming the mental health system.

And suddenly, people started trusting the *New York World*.

Nellie Bly's investigative journalism paved the way for the subscriber era. Newspapers started doubling down on deeper coverage, better stories, and specialized topics. This gave birth to the magazine industry, and led both Pulitzer and Hearst to become two of the most famous names in the history of journalism.

We learn a couple of things from this story. First, when content is everywhere, it pays to go deep.

Second, we once again see the pattern:

The newspapers printed the news (create), handed it out for a penny on street corners (connect), and learned that sensational headlines worked best (optimize).

So then they printed sensational stories (create), handed them out the same way (connect), and realized that they weren't building loyalty (optimize).

So then they hired investigative journalists and went deep into specific topics (create), got subscribers and delivered to them (connect), doubled down on what worked (optimize), and changed the world.

Now let's fast-forward another 200 years to the fastest-growing media company in history.

You might remember Upworthy, the do-gooder website launched in 2012 by a couple of clever, socially minded

Internet journalists. Upworthy built an incredibly large audience by simply going through the steps of our flywheel pattern faster than any publisher in history.

Upworthy's strategy was to take an inspirational video someone else had already created but no one paid attention to. It would then repackage this story on a nicely designed article page with a new headline, eye-catching photo, and enticing introduction (create) and share the new version with a few people on Facebook (connect).

Then Upworthy would see whether the new version of the story had more engagement than the old version of the story (optimize). Did people read or watch the whole thing? Did they share it?

Based on that research, Upworthy would test dozens of versions of these stories. They'd create new headlines and photos and share them with new groups of people on Facebook until it had came up with the optimal headline and the perfect image (create) to give the story the best shot at going viral. And then Upworthy would send the optimized version of the story to everyone it knew via email (connect).

Using this strategy, Upworthy grew five times faster than any other media company in history—all because it went through the flywheel faster than anyone else.

But there's a cautionary tale here, too. After a few years of growth, Upworthy's traffic plummeted when the company stopped using the flywheel process effectively.

There were a couple of reasons. First, Facebook changed its algorithm to punish Upworthy-style content, after dozens of copycats that began using its most successful headline styles.

This meant Upworthy took a big traffic hit overnight. And instead of optimizing around this change—finding a better way to connect with audiences than through Facebook or adapting its content creation strategy further—Upworthy failed to adapt.

Upworthy's slip from the top of the traffic charts is illustrative, too. That's because while every good storytelling operation uses some version of the flywheel (create, connect, optimize) to build its audience, the best never stop reinventing their approach.

Want to know the great news? Today's technology makes it possible for you to do this more effectively than ever before. Before the Internet, you had to own a printing press and delivery trucks and a staff of newspaper boys in order to create, connect, and optimize. But today, you can do all of this with a laptop and an Internet connection.

But now that we know the flywheel, the real challenge begins. How do we get the most out of it?

Connect: The Storytelling Bull's-Eye

How you plan to reach your audience is an important factor when figuring out what you should create. So we're going to dig into the second step of the flywheel strategy first: connect.

For every year that passes between us writing this and you reading this book, the Internet will have birthed a half-dozen new media platforms (or who knows how many more). There are new ways to connect with audiences every day, so we can't tell you exactly where to put your content tomorrow. But what we can do is tell you that the new rules of media present brands and upstart publishers with perhaps the greatest relationship-building opportunity in history.

That's because it's cheaper and easier to reach people than ever been before. Before the Internet, if you wanted to get your stories in people's hands, you had to pay for tons of infrastructure. If you wanted to launch a newspaper to distribute text stories, you needed to buy a printing press, hire delivery trucks and deliverymen, and make deals with newspaper stands. If you wanted to distribute video content, you either needed millions of dollars to launch a TV station or you had to license that content to an existing station and give up all control. You were at the mercy of the gatekeepers.

Thanks to YouTube and Facebook and Twitter and Medium and Instagram and every other social platform, however, there is now no cost to publish on a global scale to billions of people. There's no gate between creators and their audience. As a result, the demand for content is exploding. Time spent with digital media tripled between 2010 and 2016, according to comScore, largely thanks to the proliferation of smartphones. Two-thirds of U.S. adults now walk around with unlimited content machines in their pockets, and that number is only expected to grow over the coming years.

In addition, the paid content distribution capabilities of social networks—Facebook, LinkedIn, and Instagram—grow more sophisticated every day. For less than 50 cents on Facebook, you can get the exact right person to read or watch any piece of content, whether that person is a mother from Idaho Falls or a health care executive in Manhattan. And when the content is really good, the cost is often just a few cents. With the right infrastructure, approach, and passion for storytelling, you have a Super Bowl–sized chance to reach millions—or focus on the tiny few who matter—every single day.

Still, things can change so fast in the social media world that it's hard to know what the right tactic will be when you read this book. What we can do, however, is give you a formula for figuring it out.

The formula is what we call the bullseye. It starts by dividing the world of companies into categories along two dimensions: audience and goal.

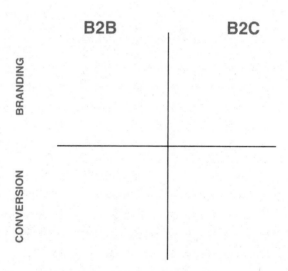

To put it crudely, there are two types of companies: B2B (businesses marketing to businesses) and B2C (businesses marketing to consumers). They generally have two categories of goals: branding (whether and how people think about you) and conversion (people taking an action, such as buying something or requesting to talk to a salesperson).

Some companies may fit in one or more of these categories, and that's fine. They may just have a bigger job to do than others.

Regardless of which category your company is in, the most powerful place to connect with an audience is on your website. Here, you control the branding and conversion experience. You can ensure that people see what you want them to see and are prompted to take the actions you want them to take.

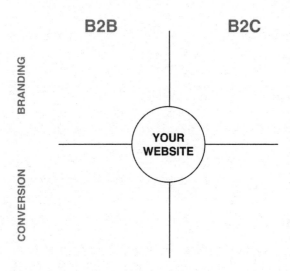

But most companies don't have everyone they want to connect with magically flocking to their website, so they need to connect with people in other ways, too.

The second most effective place to connect is on the audience's home turf: their email. This also works across the four categories of companies. When you send an email, you control most of the branding and most of the conversion experience. It comes from you and goes right to the receiver's inbox.

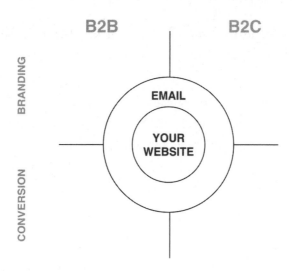

If you don't have your target audience's email addresses, you need to compel them to come to you. This means you need to catch their eye in the places they spent their time online.

So where does your audience hang out? What social networks? What websites? What social channels? What apps?

The category that your company fits into will help determine this. If you're a B2B company interested in brand, your best strategy at the time of this writing would probably be to reach people on LinkedIn, Facebook, YouTube, and podcasts. If you're B2B and interested in conversions, you'll probably aim for Google Search, SlideShare, or relevant companies' email lists.

If you're doing branding for B2C, you may shoot for many of the same places as B2B but skip LinkedIn in favor of Instagram and Reddit. If you're B2C and after conversions, you'll want to head to Pinterest and Instagram.

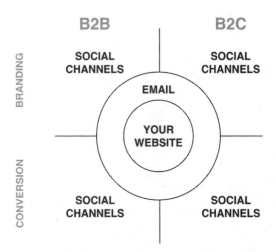

The channels where you plan to connect with your audience will help you determine what type of content to create. The stories you tell should fit those channels.

The strategy from here is simple. Every story should bring the audience at least one step closer to the center of the bull's-eye. Your LinkedIn posts or YouTube videos ought to tell people to subscribe for more content via email. And that great content in your emails should drive people to your website again and again.

Once again, the platforms will change as years go by, but the principle behind this methodology shouldn't.

(We dig into the nitty-gritty of this strategy in our *Content Marketing Methodology* e-book. Check it out at http://contently.com/resources if you're interested in exploring this further.)

Once you have a general strategy for how to connect, it's time to figure out what stories to create.

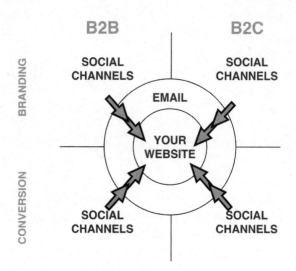

Create: The Story Funnel-Matrix

In the same way that the parameters of a haiku make it easier to write a poem on the fly, the parameters of the following diagram are helpful for coming up with the stories that you'll be using to connect with people in the ways we just explained.

We call this haiku strategy the funnel-matrix.

The funnel-matrix has two dimensions. The first maps loosely to the stages of a typical marketing funnel: awareness, consideration, and acquisition. In turn, these map loosely to our Bullseye: When your audience is spending time on a certain channel online, you're trying to get them to pay attention to you. When you manage to catch your audience's attention, you're trying to get them to consider doing business with you. And by the time you get them to talk to your salespeople, you want to acquire their business.

What stories you tell will depend on your current relationship with your audience—where you are as a couple, to use the obligatory marketing-dating analogy.

When you first meet someone, your conversations tend to be around things that you have in common—your shared interests and values. This is why so many people make small talk about the weather. It affects everyone, so it's something we all have in common.

You probably won't dive into your health problems the first time you meet someone. You probably won't share intimate details about the people in your life.

But after you meet, you might start sharing some of those things, especially if the first date goes well. You might start to paint a picture of your dream life: where you want to live, your ideal career, where you want to travel. Though you shouldn't hit them with a marriage proposal at this point, you'll start to share more about yourself—what you care about and what you want.

By the third or fourth date, you'll naturally be sharing more personal stories than before. This is the way a relationship progresses. (Notice how storytelling is such a big part of what we do when we're dating. It's good for more than just marketing and publishing!)

This brings us back to our storytelling funnel-matrix. In the beginning of a relationship, you should tell stories about shared interests and values. As things progress, you can tell stories about the people in your life (like your customers or employees). Finally, as things start getting more serious, you tell stories about your products and services themselves.

The second dimension of the funnel-matrix adds an extra bit of planning help to your content creation strategy. This comes straight from the playbook of newsrooms.

The idea is to divide the stories you tell into three more categories based on time: timely stories that are pertinent based on news or current events; seasonal stories that are relevant because of the time of year; and evergreen stories that will be valuable no matter when the audience sees or hears them.

Take our client American Express, for example. Amex's OPEN line of credit cards wants small business owners to know that they care about them. Building that trust is a key element of their B2B branding, so they tell stories in various places, most notably on OPEN Forum, a content hub and newsletter that attracts millions of small business owners each month. They're mostly interested in staying top of mind, not driving conversions or talking about Amex's products.

Instead, they tell stories about how small business owners handle challenges like hiring and growth. These are examples of *evergreen stories*.

Sometimes OPEN Forum spots something relevant that happens in the news and writes stories about how it affects small business owners, like new overtime laws and tax policies. These are *timely + top-funnel stories*.

And one day a year, American Express sponsors a holiday called Small Business Saturday, where it encourages consumers to shop at local businesses instead of big ones. To promote the upcoming holiday, Amex creates videos about small businesses around the country that are making a difference in their communities. These are *seasonal stories*.

Shinola's stories of its factory workers and their mission to transform Detroit are about both values (saving American jobs) and its company/people. So they are *evergreen + top/mid-funnel*.

GE Reports, which tells stories of how GE invents really cool products (but doesn't try to get you to buy those products), are mid-funnel and often timely—as the company reports on new innovations—but also evergreen because many of the stories are still interesting after the news is over.

The Groupon stories we talked about fit into the category of timely + bottom-funnel. They're stories about product deals Groupon wants you to buy on one specific day.

Zady's stories about the Indigo Skinny Jeans are evergreen + bottom-funnel. They'll be around whenever you are ready for them.

The smartest brand storytellers are constantly on the lookout for data to tell them what their audiences are interested in during each stage of the funnel and each segment of the Bullseye. They obsess over it. And that's because they know it's their secret advantage.

Optimize: Cranking the Efficiency

Our favorite way of explaining the last step of the flywheel involves the one thing that Joe loves talking about more than content: basketball.

There's a good chance you already know who basketball legend LeBron James is. But unless you're a basketball geek like Joe, you may not know about the man behind James's run to four consecutive NBA Finals with the Miami Heat. James and his teammates owe their outsize success in large part to their smart, data-crazy young coach, Erik Spoelstra.

When James joined the team in 2010, he and superstar teammates Dwyane Wade and Chris Bosh struggled to play cohesively. They had great talent but suffered surprising defeats together. The losses were so bad during James's first season on the Heat that sportswriters openly wondered if the team was doomed.

What James and his teammates needed, it turned out, was not to learn to play well—they were already great players individually—but how to adapt their playing style together as they faced each unique opponent.

Coach Spoelstra was the one who got them thinking about this the right way—and he used data to do it. When the early losses piled up, Spoelstra didn't pressure the team president into making a hasty trade and shipping one of his stars away.

Instead, the young coach turned to advanced statistics to understand what went wrong when the Heat lost to different types of teams—and what they could do differently.

To the casual observer, the Heat didn't appear to be a drastically different team between their first and second year, but those who studied the intricacies of the game saw just how important Spoelstra's adjustments were. He got the team to play an aggressive, unorthodox style of defense that complemented their athletic yet undersized roster. On offense, he turned one-on-one gridlock into a system of spacing that opened up corner three-pointers, which is widely considered the most efficient shot in basketball since it's worth 3-points yet comes from a distance of just 22 feet.

The story of the Heat's dominant run usually focuses on James, but in many ways, the unsung star was Spoelstra—the nerdy, lanky coach who would blend right in at a marketing conference. He understood that basketball strategy is not one-size-fits-all. He used smart analytics to do what other coaches didn't as well: tweak his players' strategy on the fly. This gave the Heat the advantage they needed to rise to the top.

To execute a successful content operation, you need to embrace your inner "Spoelstra." (Shane thinks we could just say "nerd" here, but Joe insists on "Spoelstra", and would like everyone to know that when Shane watches sports, he asks questions like, "Do the bad guys have the ball now?") Because for all the talk about big data, many marketers still struggle to translate numbers into action. Part of that struggle is not knowing which metrics matter, and part is not doing the work on a daily basis to create the most successful content possible by looking hard at those metrics.

If the Heat were coached by a stubborn, old-school coach who insisted on building an offense around secretly-inefficient shots, like long two-pointers, there's a good chance James would have left South Beach without a title. Likewise, brands that stubbornly stick to their preconceived content strategies will never reach their full potential.

The good news is that it's easier than ever to make smart, data-driven decisions with content. When armed with the right tools and an understanding of how to measure content to reflect your goals, you can create a powerful system that drives your content forward.

The third step of the flywheel is the thing that makes the difference between contenders and champions. It's about adjusting the previous two steps (create and connect) through smart analysis.

The simple way to describe the process is to look at the stories that did well, figure out the common elements of those stories, and do more of those things.

We like to use the analogy of a never-ending horse race. Take 10 horses and make them race. Then take the two horses that won, and get them to make more horses. Have all those horses race, and repeat.

But how do you decide what a winning story looks like? What content metrics really matter?

This is probably the question we are asked the most. We love the way this question is phrased because it sounds like we're deliberating the Oscars.

Which metric really mattered this year, Joe?

Well, I'd say brand awareness has had a tremendous impact on our cultural consciousness, wouldn't you?

Right now, there's a temptation in content marketing to divide metrics into two camps: useless and magical. But when it comes to content analytics, there are no absolutes.

We're big believers of the BuzzFeed theory that all data are useful, and there's no "magic metric." In the words of BuzzFeed's former director of data science, Ky Harlin, "You're almost better off doing nothing than focusing on just one single metric because you're just very prone to false conclusions."

Here's another thing that will lead you to false conclusions: not knowing why you're even creating content in the first place.

According to the Content Marketing Institute's 2016 and 2017 research, nearly two-thirds of marketers create content without any documented strategy, and more than half of both B2B and B2C marketers are not sure what a successful content program looks like. This is the biggest problem in content marketing right now. You can't figure out what analytics matter the most if you don't know what you want to achieve with your content.

Your company's business goals should determine your content objectives, which should, in turn, determine the key performance indicators (KPIs) you measure. Here's a sample chart from the "Content Methodology Best Practices Report" Joe wrote with analyst Rebecca Lieb:

Business Goal	Content Objectives	KPIs
Educational	**Grow brand awareness:** Establish a lasting position in the marketplace by building an engaged audience for the brand.	• Total attention time • Total people • Total social actions • Avg. finish per engaged story • Avg. people per engaged story • Views across social platforms • Engagement rate • Share of voice • Earned media
	Thought leadership: Build a reputation as a trusted leader with industry-leading expertise that serves as a differentiating factor.	• Influencer mentions/ shares • Share of voice • Share of search • Top keywords • Content citation/syndication • Avg. stories per person • Total attention time • Total people • Total social actions • Avg. finish per engaged story • Avg. people per engaged story • Engagement rate
	Brand sentiment: Improve the opinion of the brand among the target audience over time.	• Sentiment by channel • Sentiment by influencer • Sentiment over time
Revenue generation	**Lead generation:** Create content that drives high-quality leads.	• Lead conversions • Avg. lead score • Sales-qualified leads (SQLs) • Opportunities • Search traffic • Return visitor rate
	Lead nurturing: Move leads through the funnel until they become customers.	• Return visit rate by SQLs • Click-through rate (CTR) of lead nurture emails • Time to conversion • Cost per customer
Customer experience	Loyalty	• Return visitor rate • Email subscription rate • Social following growth • Avg. pieces of content read by current customers
	Customer service	• Number of service issues resolved using digital content and tools • Rating of service tools

If you're mostly concerned with brand awareness metrics, you want to closely examine how engaged people are with the content you produce.

We're spoiled by having access to Contently Analytics, which measures a lot of the user engagement metrics that Google Analytics does not, but here are some of our personal favorites:

Engaged readers
The number of people who spend at least 15 seconds with a piece of content.

Shares
Still important. When people go out of their way to share your content with their social network, that means something.

Average attention time
The average amount of time someone spends scrolling, clicking, highlighting, and generally paying attention to your content. (In other words, not just leaving the tab open while they microwave a Hot Pocket—no disrespect to Hot Pockets.)

Average finish
How far are people getting through your story? If they're bouncing at the 25 percent mark, you likely have a misleading headline or a bad lede. If they're finishing 90 percent of the story on average, you did something right.

Social lift
A simple calculation—(shares/views + 1)—that tells you how much extra organic social traffic a story is likely to get, which will help you prioritize distribution.

Average stories per person
Are people sticking around to read more than one story?

Press score
A score that basically weight-ranks press mentions earned by content based on how relevant that publication is to your target audience, and how prevalent the mention is. One of the biggest reasons that we invest heavily in original research is that it gets us a lot of press from major outlets, like our in-depth study on consumer perception of native

advertising we published with CUNY in December 2016. It's huge when Digiday features our research and that would mention get a highly weighted press score. If the study gets a passing mention in NYCDoggies.com, that would earn a lower ranking—no disrespect to NYCDoggies.com.

If you're concerned about lead generation, you still want to examine engagement metrics—as we noted above, someone's not likely to marry you (or buy something from you) after the first date. Your odds of "converting" (for love or profit) are much higher after you've built a relationship with them. But there are additional metrics that will help you figure out how well your content is contributing to lead generation.

Email conversion rate

One of the best indicators of a great story is when it convinces the audience to sign up for our newsletter.

Lead form conversion rate

When it convinces them to express interest in expensive software, even better.

Lead score

Based on a number of factors (company size, title, industry, and other information) how likely the lead is to convert into a customer.

Opportunities

Folks who enter our marketing funnel inbound through content and express interest in becoming a customer to one of our salespeople. At Contently, for instance, more than 50 percent of our opportunities are sourced organically

from people reading our content or downloading an
e-book.

We could go on and on. Choosing your favorite content
metric is like choosing your favorite Teenage Mutant Ninja
Turtle. Although if we told our 10-year-old selves that in 20
years, the Teenage Mutant Ninja Turtles would be replaced in
our lives by content metrics, they'd probably cry. And then
they'd tell you that our favorite Ninja Turtle is Raphael, no
questions asked.

Another best practice, as we mentioned previously, is to tag
your story (by topic, persona, format, etc.) and compare production metrics to performance metrics. That way, you can see
which stories are under- or overperforming against your KPIs.
Essentially, you can create dozens of different horse races,
figure out the winner, and alter your content strategy accordingly. These are the types of insights we need to be armed with
when our CEO emails us and asks why we just published a
quiz challenging people to figure out whether a headline is
about Pokémon Go or Kim Kardashian. (Which, not surpris-
ingly, was one of our most popular stories of the summer of
2016—it was a strange, much more innocent time.)

That brings us to another important point. Often, the
value of this process is as much in improving the quality of
your content as reporting your success up the chain of command and getting more resources to do more ambitious
content.

We'd recommend using your data to tell a short, visual story
about your content success. Pick out three or four data points
that showcase how your content efforts help the business. Show

progress. Communicate that information in a few different ways. Send an email. Plug it into Slack. Ask to present for 10 minutes at your next all-hands meeting. Sure, you might be annoying, but you'll also get to keep your job.

It also helps if you have the same first name as your CEO. People come up to our CEO Joe Coleman all the time to praise *The Content Strategist,* thinking that he's Joe Lazauskas. (Coleman's a superanalytical guy, but we secretly suspect that's why he keeps our edit team.) In all seriousness, though, specific instances of positive feedback are always helpful. If clients and prospects love your content and say so, make sure you let your senior leadership know. That's what the "forward" button is there for.

6 The Brand Newsroom

I t's 9 a.m. on a July morning in Reebok's newsroom, and a brainstorming session called "Binge Think," is heating up.

When we walk in, Dan Mazei, the senior director of Reebok's Global Newsroom, is standing on a chair, scribbling story ideas on a whiteboard. A dozen staffers surround him, gathered on couches and colorful footrests. Everyone is young and fit, and we feel like we've walked on the set of an office comedy. The banter that follows confirms these suspicions.

"Refinery29 headline yesterday: 'The Magical Advice We Got from a Real Fitness Witch.'"

"A witch?"

"Yes, a fitness witch. She works at Enchantments, an occult shop in Manhattan. She was also a trainer at Equinox."

"Puts the whole fitness goth trend into a whole new light."

"There's a fitness goth trend?"

"Oh my god, yeah. People work out in all black. There's a studio on Bowery. Can you search for it? It has a bondage spinning bike on the ceiling."

"So, she can be our goth fitness expert?"

The exercise goes on like this for an hour. By the end, Mazei stands on his tiptoes, using every inch of available whiteboard space. The team settles on a plan to shoot a video two days later with an influential 15-year-old power lifter. They'll give him old-school toys like a Skip-It and see how he reacts to bygone devices once meant for Millennials.

The team also decides on a half dozen blog posts—ranging from indoor fitness routines to help you survive the heat wave to a scary interview with a former Spice Girl.

As they break into their respective pods, the team seems energized. We're left staring at the whiteboard, marveling at how similar this "brand newsroom" is to the hippest (and most successful) "traditional" newsrooms in modern media.

The Talent Race

Not long ago, the term *brand newsroom* sounded like an oxymoron. But as interruptive advertising grew more taboo, large corporations began taking a cue from media outlets on ways to connect with target audiences. Seventy-eight percent of CMOs at last count said that content—storytelling!—was the future of marketing. In turn, many have started to build in-house content teams like Reebok's.

But to build a brand newsroom that can crank out top-performing content, brands have had to compete with traditional publishing machines to draw in the best creative talent. Initially, this was difficult because many creative people still had their sights set on careers at traditional media outlets. There was a huge difference, in a lot of film and journalism school graduates' minds, between working at Vice versus Deutsche Bank.

However, as brands developed newsrooms that mimic the open environment of hip publishers like BuzzFeed and Vice, that migration is picking up.

You get a sense of creative freedom in Reebok's plush, brightly lit newsroom, where Binge Think sessions give it an unmistakable "startup" vibe. There's a freedom to pitch any idea, no matter how ludicrous, and a genuine emphasis on great storytelling over marketing gobbledygook.

The sessions were started by Mazei, who came from Edelman PR in late 2015 to head Reebok's content efforts in the hope of inspiring greater flexibility. "[You have] to be able to pivot on a dime. To embrace creativity," he told us. "It's a helpful dynamic for the way that we operate as a newsroom because we're not supposed to be heads down at a desk."

Reebok's newsroom strategy is a way for the brand to reinvent itself in a media-centric world and differentiate from its competitors. Instead of competing head-to-head with Nike or Under Armour for big-name athlete endorsements, it has focused its energy on nurturing relationships with niche communities—through stories.

Reebok's newsroom spends a lot of time in particular telling stories for CrossFit junkies, because the brand sponsors the CrossFit Games. This content strategy helps Reebok stay connected to CrossFit devotees in between competitions.

"Our brand ethos is that we have stepped completely to a different direction," Mazei said. "We're [trying to reach] the person who's in the gym five times a week, working out hard, doing the tough stuff."

To connect with this niche audience, the apparel brand decided to stop thinking like marketers and start thinking like a publisher.

The Virtual Newsroom

Building a newsroom can be a big commitment. Between office space, renovations, and full-time employees, the costs can really add up.

The good news is that it's entirely possible today to have a newsroom without big fixed costs. For every Nestlé and Reebok that builds a mini-BuzzFeed inside its headquarters, there's a brand building a newsroom that, for the most part, doesn't exist in a physical space.

That's something we've witnessed firsthand at Contently. Hundreds of brands use our platform to build teams of editors, writers, designers, and videographers and manage their content operations completely virtually. They build remote teams, manage The Flywheel using software, and communicate via chat, FaceTime, or phone.

For folks like David Gardner, SoFi's former director of content marketing, this arrangement was just logical. "Because we didn't have writers in house, we tapped Contently's freelance network," Gardner said. "We also needed a managing editor to scale content and manage writers."

Or take Genpact, a business transformation firm, which used Contently to quickly spin up a global newsroom with dozens of writers without having to endure the laborious process of building an internal team.

A virtual brand newsroom built through a software platform makes a lot of sense. Freelancers get paid well while working from the comfort of their homes. Brands quickly build and maintain a newsroom without having to recruit full-time employees, which lets them creatively use budgets that otherwise wouldn't be earmarked for personnel. The virtual model would have been difficult to pull off years ago, but advances in content marketing technology make it an increasingly attractive option.

What Type of Newsroom Do You Prefer?

For brands that want to be heard, an investment in content is inevitable. According to the Content Marketing Institute's 2017 benchmark reports, 89 percent of B2B marketers and 86 percent of B2C marketers now do content for marketing purposes. And more than 40 percent of marketers in both groups say their content marketing budgets will increase.

In the process, we'll likely see a few different models emerge. Some—like Reebok, JPMorgan Chase, and Casper—will build internal newsrooms that resemble the headquarters of digital publishers. Others, like Genpact and SoFi, will leverage content technology and tap into networks of freelance creative talent. Then there will be companies like Marriott, which has physical brand newsrooms all over the world but also runs a travel magazine staffed by freelancers and uses content marketing technology to connect global teams.

For years, "brand newsroom" has been one of the most lampooned marketing buzzwords. But in the future, the pressure to source and maintain top talent is resulting in some exciting and unexpected new content marketing models. Brands will have to decide what's right for them based on their culture, budgets, and resources. But one thing's for certain: There are more attractive options than ever before.

In other words, as storytelling becomes a bigger and bigger deal for all of our companies, the barriers to doing more of it are being wiped away.

7 The Future of Brand Storytelling

I n 1956, a dust of mysterious plant spores blew into the town of Santa Mira, California. That's when things started getting weird.

Big green pods started growing around town. But even stranger, local psychiatrists suddenly had an influx of visits from community members. Each patient suffered from a condition called Capgras delusion—where you believe someone you know is no longer him- or herself. Soon the doctors started panicking, too; their own friends and family members had also begun acting weird. They walked around, staring blankly like zombies.

Before long, an epidemic of mass hysteria broke out.

It turns out that the doctors' patients were right. Their loved ones had been replaced.

By aliens.

The plant spores had come from outer space, and the pods had been consuming people while they slept, regenerating identical copies of them in the night. Personality-less zombie copies.

In no time, almost everyone in Santa Mira had turned into a Pod Person. A thousand versions of the same empty shell wandered the streets.

This never happened, of course. It's the plot of the classic movie *Invasion of the Body Snatchers*.

But it is exactly what might happen to the craft of business storytelling if we aren't careful.

The zombiefication has already started. Millions of smart marketers have been infected by the content bug. They've bought into the idea that stories and education build relationships and make people care in ways that commercial sales pitches and calls-to-action do not. This is a good thing! But, unfortunately, because content is hard, many have started drifting asleep and doing the same thing as everyone else. Or worse—dressing up the same old intrusive advertising tactics and calling it storytelling.

This might sound a little pessimistic. There is truly a lot of great storytelling going on in the business world. But the warning signs are clear.

At Contently, we get thousands of inbound requests every month from businesses that want help with content. We work with hundreds of the world's top brand publishers and help them create and manage content marketing. And our blog reports more regular news coverage of the brand content industry than just about any other publication. With this view of the landscape and what's coming up on the horizon, we see zombie content as the biggest challenge for brand publishers moving forward.

Two forces are bringing this about. First, the brand content industry is starting to get saturated. It's like when the Internet made it so anyone could record their own music and publish it for free online. Before long, an insane amount of music had flooded the Internet. A lot of it was bad or boring. (We'd include links to our own bands' old Myspace pages if it wasn't so embarrassing!) After a while, it became hard to find a good new artist among the Myspace zombies.

The second thing is a lot of vendors that aren't that good at content are selling zombie pods. Agencies that specialize in other things throw the word *content* in their same old offerings. "Me too" tech vendors. Publishers with branded content studios that use the publisher's reputation but do shabby work. The output: zombie content.

Based on all of our reporting and research and by doing content ourselves, tomorrow's brands must do three big things to not become Pod People and actually get results from their storytelling efforts.

The future, we believe, belongs to those who get the following right.

#1: Breakthrough Quality Storytelling

At the turn of the twentieth century, Thomas Edison unveiled a brand new invention that would change the world. It was the kinetoscope, the first practical device that could display moving pictures. Essentially, it was a film projector.

With the release of his kinetoscope and its subsequent updates, Edison would ceremoniously host events to screen motion pictures. Some of these early films can be found in online archives today. They were crude by today's standards, but back then they were miraculous.

On one such occasion in 1903, people in New York City dressed up and gathered for a special Edison film—the latest and greatest. They put on tuxedos and gowns. They stood in line outside the theater house. And then they sat down as the lights dimmed. As the moving pictures began, people gasped. The black-and-white images were so lifelike.

The film was of three men on a trash barge, shoveling.

That's it. Just shoveling trash for five minutes.

The movie was literally garbage.

Can you imagine? People bought furs in anticipation of this screening. They argued about who would babysit the children. They drank brandy and champagne and sat in fancy seats . . . to watch garbage.

They were willing to do so because the medium itself was so novel. Motion pictures were so cool that people would show up to watch anything. Even garbage.

But that didn't last long. In the first decade of the twentieth century, the U.S. film industry produced 23 films. In the next decade, it produced more than 4,000. Then nearly 7,000 in the following.

And then the number of films made each decade dropped sharply. By the 1960s, only a couple hundred movies were being made per year.

That's because garbage isn't really that interesting unless it's new. After a while, people stopped going to watch bad movies, so fewer people invested in making them.

The film industry learned that it wasn't enough to just make a movie. In order for people to turn out to the theater, the movie had to have a good story.

Things really turned around in the 1970s with the birth of the blockbuster. *Star Wars*, *The Godfather*, and others gave people compelling stories that broke through the noise of everything else competing for their attention, like the news, TV shows, and screaming kids.

With every new way of communicating with an audience, the same pattern has emerged. We're always excited by the latest thing, whether it's radio, the Internet, or Snapchat, and we pay attention, even if it's garbage. But eventually, we lose interest in content for content's sake on these platforms, and, ultimately, we want awesome content—or we'll find something else to do.

Today's content marketing situation is similar. Brands publishing blog posts, infographics, and social videos was novel, but it's not anymore. Which is why the future belongs to brands that create the kind of content that's so much better than what's out there that no one can accuse them of being zombies.

This is, not coincidentally, exactly what happened with the whole Myspace thing. Once anyone could produce music and put it on the Internet themselves, the Internet exploded with zombie tunes. Soon, a regular YouTube video of someone playing a guitar was not interesting. It became the stuff of the Pod People. That is, until—and we can't believe we're saying this—Justin Bieber came along. When Bieber was 13, music marketer Scooter Braun accidentally clicked on one of Bieber's acoustic guitar home videos. Braun was impressed and brought Bieber to Atlanta to meet Usher.

Bieber soon became a star. So have many others like him. They were people who never would have been discovered, but they took destiny into their own hands by creating content that stood out amid the garbage.

In the 1970s, blockbuster movies came about because of two things: visionary directors who created amazing stories and improved filmmaking and special effects technology.

Tomorrow's business storyteller will think of themselves as the director, the Steven Spielberg or Kathryn Bigelow, sent to craft the stories that are 10 times better than the zombie competition—as long as they have a coherent plan. Which brings us to our next key . . . .

#2: Rigorously Strategic

Every September, tens of thousands of marketers and other business people gather in Cleveland, Ohio, for a business storytelling conference called Content Marketing World. For the past couple of years, there's a chart that pops up in presentation after presentation. It looks like this:

Google Search interest over time: Content Marketing

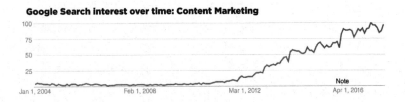

This chart shows the explosive growth of searches on Google for the term "content marketing," the umbrella term for the larger industry that focuses on business storytelling. People at Content Marketing World love this chart. It's basically their version of the "Everything Is Awesome" theme song from *The Lego Movie*. (Which was the Greatest Content Marketing Program Ever™, as anyone at Content Marketing World will tell you.)

While this chart is interesting—and a great snapshot of the booming interest in business storytelling—it doesn't tell the full story. While most companies have now accepted that great storytelling is crucial if you want to break through in a noisy digital world, a lot of them have experienced serious growing pains as they've tried to integrate storytelling into their businesses.

In fact, they've experienced a lot of the same challenges that the early filmmakers did. In particular, a lot of their stories haven't been very good. They've run into the same garbage problem as our early Edison copycats.

This is extremely common for new marketing disciplines. Gartner, one of the most trusted analyst firms, captures this in the "Hype Cycle," which maps the evolution of new marketing technologies and disciplines. And it tells a much fuller and more interesting story than the Search Trends chart on the previous page. As of this writing, the last Gartner Hype Cycle was published in November 2016. And look where content marketing falls—smack dab in what Gartner calls the trough of disillusionment (see below).

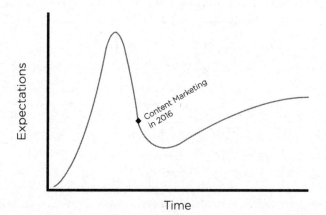

The "trough of disillusionment" is probably the most existentially depressing term in marketing we've ever heard. The worst part is that new industries can't really avoid it. First, everyone gets superexcited based on fawning tech blogger reports, advertising magazine trend stories, and prophetic thought leadership from charming founders who are leading the way. A few early-adopters see massive success as hype builds. But then everyone joins the party, so resistance and roadblocks crop up at every step, especially at large organizations. Brands need to wait as vendors scramble to meet their needs. Expectations fade and disillusionment sets in.

Basically, everyone gets sad and frustrated.

The start of content marketing's hype cycle, in 2012, shouldn't have surprised anyone. By then, it'd become clear that consumers were spending less time paying attention to traditional advertising. Instead of watching TV commercials, they were streaming advertising-free shows on Netflix and HBO Go or locked in on their smartphones. Instead of getting news from print newspapers, they were reading whatever their friends shared on Facebook. Publishers, desperate to stay afloat, choked web pages with display units, until display had begun to feel less like a channel and more like one of the 10 plagues.

Then along came content marketing, which posed a simple solution: What if brands just told stories that people wanted to watch, hear, and read?

The early examples were inspiring. Red Bull pioneered the idea of a brand as a media company, while early Contently clients such as GE, American Express, and Mint showed that

B2B organizations and companies in niche industries could get in on the fun as well.

In response, brands started building content teams and earmarking experimental budgets for content marketing. In hindsight, this was the wrong approach. Instead of serving as the fuel for a brand's entire marketing operation, content often existed in a vacuum. Brands would launch a flashy blog hidden in the recesses of a corporate website and just expect it to work. Even if that content got little paid or organic promotion, audiences were supposed to find it anyway.

It's easy to see why this happened. Few organizations had any sort of documented content strategy—and more than 60 percent of marketers still don't. Since the digital age changed human behavior so fast, marketers couldn't draw from established education or instruction. Savvy marketers at the companies we've highlighted in this book—Marriott, Mint, American Express, Chase, Dollar Shave Club, GE, and others—figured out how to make storytelling the heart of their business and crushed the competition. They built brand newsrooms that told amazing stories and engaged the audiences that mattered to their brand.

But others had a much steeper learning curve. And many decided to simply build a blog and pray that people just showed up like Kevin Costner's ghost friends in *Field of Dreams*. After all, it was a hell of a lot easier than figuring out how to put together a real strategy that would work.

This has resulted in a stark difference in success between the blockbuster brands that got ahead and mastered brand storytelling early, and most companies, which struggled to transform their business and adapt. A 2016 study by Beckon, a marketing data firm, for instance, revealed that the top 5 percent of branded content accounted for 90 percent of all engagement.

Does this mean that content marketing no longer works?

To the contrary, it validates something obvious—that if you create something original and great, you have the opportunity to monopolize consumer attention and leave your competitors in the shadows. It's proof that mediocre content just isn't effective.

However, based on what we've seen over the last couple of years covering the industry and helping hundreds of Contently clients develop breakthrough content strategies, that gap is closing. We are about to move past the trough of disillusionment. And that's because brands are finally realizing that great content has to be integrated into every part of their marketing and communications strategy. And to pull that off, those brands have realized that they need something crucial.

They need the technology advantage. Which brings us to our third key to the future of brand storytelling.

#3: Tech-Enabled and Data-Optimized

In 2011, the streaming video service Netflix decided to make a new original TV series for the first time. Until that point, the company had simply bought licenses to stream movies and television shows that other companies had made.

The show was a political drama called *House of Cards*, based on a British show with the same name. It would star the award-winning Kevin Spacey and be directed by David

Fincher, director of *The Social Network* and other blockbuster movies.

It was a big investment. TV shows cost a lot of money, and this one in particular—between Spacey, Fincher, and the rest of the cast—was billed at $100 million for two seasons.

But unlike most television show decisions made through the experience and gut intuition of executives, Netflix had a secret weapon that all but ensured the investment would be worth it.

Most television and movie studios only know a few things about how well their work is received. They know how many people bought theater tickets and DVDs, and they see the reviews from critics and websites like Rotten Tomatoes. But Netflix knows a lot more. Because viewers watch through Netflix's apps, the company knows exactly how many people make it all the way through all of its movies and shows. It knows when people pause, when they rewind, and what they watch next. It knows not only what percentage of people who start *Parks and Recreation* are likely to watch several seasons, but it also knows exactly what percentage of *Parks and Recreation* fans also like, say, *Batman*.

Through its data, Netflix knew three things: People who watch Kevin Spacey movies tend to watch all the way to the end; people who watch David Fincher movies tend to watch lots of David Fincher movies; and people who watched the British *House of Cards* tended to watch it all at once and all the way through.

(Note: Just as this book was going to press it was announced that after six blockbuster seasons, Netflix planned to cancel House of Cards due to allegations of misconduct by Spacey. What Netflix's data didn't tell them was how many skeletons their star had in his closet—only that people were eager to watch his stuff back in 2011. Our guess: Netflix's future data will show a lot fewer people watching Spacey films.)

With these data, it didn't seem so crazy for Netflix to make the new *House of Cards*. And guess what? Based on the number of new subscribers Netflix picked up because of the show, the company's $100 million bet paid off in under three months, according to analysis by the *Atlantic*.

Since then, Netflix has used the same data-driven approach to green light lots of new shows: *Orange Is the New Black*, *Making a Murderer*, *Jessica Jones*, and *Stranger Things*, among others.

In regular television, it's well known that almost two-thirds of new shows will not be popular enough to get a second season. Netflix's original shows get renewed at twice the rate of regular TV, and only 30 percent of Netflix originals are canceled after one season.

Netflix's programs perform twice as well as the rest of the television market because of the way it uses technology and data. Its story also demonstrates a nice lesson for brands: If you can create content that speaks to a specific audience, you can attract the kind of subscribers who can keep you in business a lot more effectively. A relatively small number of superloyal subscribers paying Netflix $8 a month is more profitable than a huge number of viewers tuning in to a commercial on CBS.

In the same way, a relatively small number of loyal readers or viewers to a brand's own content can be worth much more to the brand than a bunch of ad impressions on some other part of the Internet.

This is the way the future will work in every content medium, not just entertainment television. The creators and companies that make smart use of data and tech will have a huge advantage over the rest.

This is only going to become truer over time, because technology is only getting better. It provides a platform on top of which content creators and distributors can operate, giving them a leg up on competition. Before long, if you're not using technology to drive decision making and efficiency, or using it to help you tell a more dynamic story, you will be less creative, less cost effective, and you will lose.

The Content Decision Engine

At Contently, the story of Netflix inspired us. And it made us think. If you had to give a name to Netflix's secret weapon, what would you call it? What would you call the amazing data that allows them to create shows that are more than twice as likely to succeed as regular network programs?

We'd call it a Content Decision Engine.

Because here's the thing: Netflix's secret weapon is more than just data. It's how they take that data and use it to gain an advantage during every part of the TV-show-creating process—from creating a strategy for the show and planning how to make it, to the actual creation of the show, to figuring out what worked and optimizing the show for the next season.

Data alone aren't very useful. You can't just show a producer a spreadsheet full of numbers and expect her to immediately know who to direct, who to cast, and what the story arc should be. By itself, data are just tiny pieces of scrap metal, far from becoming an engine. But when you have the right technology and the right assembly line of processes in place, all of those pieces of data can turn into something powerful.

This next section is for readers who are looking for an advanced guide to using technology to build a powerful storytelling operation—particularly within a large organization. It's about how to use technology to build a Content Decision Engine that'll help you make decisions faster and smarter, and gain hundreds of tiny advantages in every stage of the storytelling process.

The Content Operating Wheel

Remember the flywheel from the previous chapter? That universal formula for building a killer audience? Well when we started building our own Content Decision Engine for our clients at Contently, we broke it out into a few more stages to better reflect how the process works inside organizations. Instead of the flywheel, we just call it The Wheel.

The Wheel has the Content Decision Engine at the center powering everything, kind of like Iron Man's core reactor. And it helps you make smarter decisions during five stages of the storytelling process.

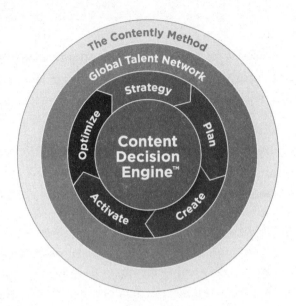

Strategy

This is when you're figuring out what kind of story your audience wants, determining how you're going to reach them, and putting together a plan of action that'll get everyone on board.

Plan

The phase when you're deciding how exactly you're going to pull off your strategy—content calendar, staffing your team, and budgeting.

Create

The fun part—the process of actually creating your story and making the right creative decisions to tell the best story possible.

Activate

The process where you get your stories out there and use them to build connections with the people that matter to you.

Optimize

The most important part—in which you figure out what worked and tweak your strategy so you do even better next time.

At Contently, we believe that the smart use of technology to make better and faster decisions at each of these stages will be the key to success moving forward—especially for readers who work at large, complex companies. So in this section, we want to give an advanced look under the hood at how we see Content Decision Engines impact the way businesses tell stories, and what it means for the future.

Strategy

Vice, *Vanity Fair*, and UBS walk into a bar . . .

Actually wait, it wasn't a bar. It was a conference room, and the goal of the meeting was unexpected. This unlikely trio—an iconic editorial fashion brand, an edgy media empire, and a financial services giant—were going to team up to engage one of the hardest audiences to reach on earth.

Late in 2014, UBS—a wealth management and investment bank that sits at number 27 on the *Forbes* Fortune 2000 list at the time of this writing—realized they had a problem. They were publishing smart thought leadership and analysis on their website. This was great for engaging investment geeks, but UBS's marketing research told them that they needed to reach a different, equally important audience. One that would never read investment articles on a bank's website.

UBS wanted to reach very wealthy Millennials and women. And when they dug into what those groups want, they found that they'd have to go way out of their comfort zone—and at times, even ditch the topic of finance all together.

The result was *Unlimited*, a site designed to appeal to the needs and intellectual curiosities of wealthy Millennials and women. It features the perspectives of everyone from Stephen Hawking to Lily Cole, and contemplates the very nature of wealth (money vs. experiences) and time (ephemeral concept vs. hard currency). Think of the site as a cheat sheet for sounding smart at a dinner party filled with rich, smart people.

Over the past two years, the site has been a huge success for the financial giant, helping them reach an audience that previously had little reason to pay attention to them or their wealth management services. But it was a big risk, and a brand can't dive into a strategy like this on a whim. No executive in their right mind will fund it. You need evidence. You need insights. And that's where technology has rapidly been playing a bigger and bigger role.

On the surface, Netflix's ability to come up with a killer strategy seems unreplicable. After all, they have access to billions of data points that no one else does, right? Truth is, we all have access to billions of data points about what people want. You just have to know how to build a Content Decision Engine that tells you what to do.

Before the age of social media, search engines, and smart-phones, we had very little insight into what kinds of stories people liked the most. But today, we know. That's because every time someone searches for a particular piece of information or a particular kind of story, it sends a signal to the world that's a topic they're interested in. The same is true for every time someone shares a story on social media—it's a signal that they read or watched something, and that it affected them enough that they wanted to share it with their friends.

Since all of this activity happens in just a few places—primarily Google, Facebook, Twitter, LinkedIn, Instagram, and Pinterest—we're able to piece together a pretty complete picture of what types of stories certain types of people like the most. And a slew of tech companies (including Contently) have worked to figure out how to take all these data and channel their inner Netflix, helping people figure out what kinds of stories are most likely to succeed.

At Contently, our process looks a little like this: First, we start with the target audience we want to reach. Next, we use a slew of homegrown and outside tools, like Facebook and LinkedIn Insights, to understand what topics they're most interested in.

Once we understand those topics, things get really interesting. Those audience insights might tell UBS, for instance, that their audience is really interested in artificial intelligence. But artificial intelligence is a huge topic. To break through, we'd want to know what about artificial intelligence interests people the most.

This is where search data come in. Using semantic search tools, we can see what specific phrases and questions that people most commonly search for a topic like artificial intelligence. We'd see that people search for things such as the "ethics of artificial intelligence" and "artificial intelligence jobs impact." That gives us a much better idea of the specific topics that are piquing the greatest interest.

From there, we can drill down even more, and analyze those specific topics across social media to understand what kind of content wins out. Are they long articles? Short articles? Videos? Infographics? Podcasts? Whitepapers? We can also see on what channels people are talking about this topic the most. Should we target people with this content on Facebook, or are they more likely to discover and share it on LinkedIn or Twitter?

Props to Kristen Poli, one of our brilliant content strategists at Contently, for developing this process and many other brilliant data-driven approaches to content strategy. The process looks something like this:

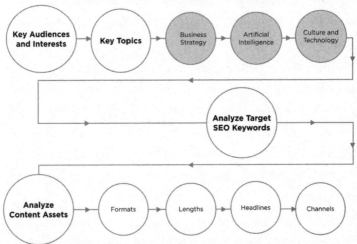

Content Decision Engine: Strategy

In the end, we have all the information we need for a great content strategy. We know what topics our audience is most interested in. We know what story format (article, video, infographic, etc.) they like the most. And we know how to reach them on both search engines and social media to make sure that they read or watch our story.

Instead of spending years laboring on reader surveys and market research, this approach allows us to figure out what will work much faster than ever before.

Plan

In 2013, two executives on the marketing team of Chase, the largest bank in the United States, decided that they wanted to push the company to double down on great storytelling. These two executives—Brian Becker and Stacey Warwick—saw what the other innovators in this book saw. That when they had great stories, it made digital marketing so much easier. And that if they wanted to continue to succeed, they'd need a way to create way more great stories than they had in the past.

But inside a giant organization like Chase in a highly regulated industry, this was going to be hard. The company had set plans and procedures, and tightly controlled budgets. Warwick and Becker had a strategy and knew what kind of content their audience wanted, but they couldn't just start creating hundreds of stories for dozens of business lines without getting buy-in first.

So, the duo did something smart. First, they started rallying support. They got allies from other departments on board with their plan for creating stories that would help each business line—small business advice for their Chase for Business line. Travel tips for their travel card members. Mortgage and budgeting advice for their mortgage lines.

Then, they got all of those people in a room and created an editorial board, chaired by their CMO, that would help plan the content they'd create. They also created a system of governance and standards so that they didn't publish anything that would get them in trouble, and so that their naturally risk-averse legal department didn't stop their plans before they got started.

"We had to set up our infrastructure and then show the organization how it could work," Becker told Contently. "We needed to prove that content can improve marketing's effectiveness. We also built standards, governance, and communication that reinforced that we would be responsible and thorough."

In the end, there were hundreds of people involved—internal teams, creative and media partners, and freelancers. The whole operation was at risk to get extremely unmanageable if they relied on traditional web technology. Never-ending email threads. Unruly spreadsheets. But that's when Chase did something smart.

Becker and Warwick were watching the rise of content marketing platforms—software build for content teams that allowed you to plan and manage our content all in one place. Create a content calendar. Set up approval workflows. Manage and approve pitches. Store all of your content and media. Staff talented freelancers to create amazing stories. All in one place.

In Chase's case, they chose Contently. It "helped as we built more structure in our organization around the newsroom and provide access to talent across different locations and topic areas," Becker said.

It worked almost immediately. They launched "News and Stories," a content hub that lived across their site and started creating dozens of stories. They saw that users who consumed those stories spent three times as much time on the site and applied for Chase products at a higher rate. Credit card applications increased by 43 percent. Customer feedback was overwhelmingly positive. They were building stronger relationships. They were building trust.

When the company relaunched its app and website in 2015, the news and stories section was front and center. It was the first thing customers saw.

From there, Chase only continued to grow. They invested in documentaries on everything from Lebron James' charity efforts to the revitalization of Brownsville, New York.

Thanks to their smart use of technology, they were able to make decisions about every piece of content they produced much quicker than they normally would. Before long, Chase was a giant company with a newsroom that operated with the speed and efficiency of a media startup.

From September 2016 to September 2017, their stories were shared almost 200,000 times—a feat totally unheard of for a bank.

More and more large organizations are accepting that great stories are the key to success for every digital channel. Before long, using technology to plan and manage this process won't be a luxury. It'll be a necessity.

Create

Remember the writers of *Avvisi*, who had to lose their heads before they could figure out the best way to create content? Or Joseph Pulitzer, who spent years publishing trash stories before he figured out that an investigative reporter like Nellie Bly was his key to success? Or our lessons from the Sludge Report, and all the work that goes into turning a mediocre story into a great one? Or the four elements of stories, and how they turned Star Wars into a blockbuster hit?

Those are all huge, complex decisions. Some took years to figure out. But what if technology could help you make them easily and instantly?

What if it could even tell you the exact emotional triggers to hit that would help your content succeed?

In 1965, two psychologists from the Air Force's research division, Ernest Tupes and Raymond Christal, developed something called The Five Factor Model, a personality classification model organized into five major traits: openness, conscientiousness, extraversion, agreeableness, and emotional range.

It was based on mapping 18,000 words in the dictionary to human traits, classifying each word into one of the five groups based on how it had been used throughout history. This revolutionary work linked language to human psychology in a scientific way like nothing before.

In other words, they cracked the code between the words you write and how people interpret those words. It can reveal the science of storytelling. The psychological response that your language as a writer evokes. The science of storytelling.

The problem was that, as a writer or editor, it's not very practical to check every sentence for its psychological effect.

But what if you could make that automatic? What if you could know the psychological traits that every story you tell triggers, and then understand whether those psychological traits make people engage with your stories more or less?

In 2016, Contently partnered with IBM Watson to do just that. We built a tone analyzer that scrapes all of the text across a website or a particular piece of text to score each of the Big Five traits on a scale of 0 to 1. You can analyze just one story, or a whole website full or stories, or all the stories from one individual writer.

As a result, you can see what kind of voice and tone your audience likes the best. You can figure out which writers resonate with them the most and what those writers do that works so well. You can create an "ideal voice and tone" for your publication and then track how well you're doing at hitting that target zone.

The brilliant engineers at Contently even built this into our text editor, too, so writers can adjust the language that they use to get a stronger response from their audience.

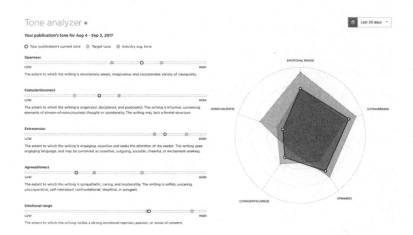

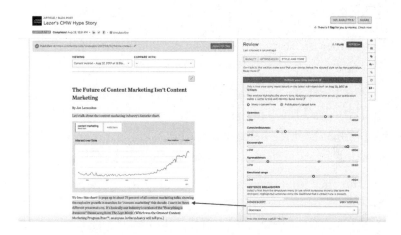

Technology will never replace the timeless art of storytelling. But it can superboost it. We believe that the storytellers of the future will master this fusion of art and science and use technology to make better, faster creative decisions.

At Contently, we've committed to building tools for storytellers to help them do this. Our story creation tools just don't tell you what voice and one to use, for instance—it also highlights the things you'd catch in a Sludge Report, like passive voice and double words. It recommends which keywords to use, which writers you should choose for a particular story, and what formats to work best.

Our goal is what yours should be, no matter what tools you're using: to spin the wheel faster and tell stories that build stronger and stronger bonds with the people you care about.

Activate

Remember the story of UBS, and how they partnered with *Vice* and *Vanity Fair* to reach wealthy Millennials?

By 2017, the site Unlimited (https://www.unlimited .world/) was a hit. Thoughtful essays on the future of business and humanity were being shared thousands of times. UBS was reaching a new audience that had barely heard of them before.

But they knew they weren't reaching their full potential. And that's when Thierry Campet, UBS's global head of marketing communications, had a breakthrough. In fact, it was the same breakthrough that we had in Chapter 4, when we were building the *The Content Strategist*.

They weren't using technology enough to breakthrough and build their audience.

So, Campet took 10 percent of his content creation budget. He put that money toward targeting readers on the channels his content analytics told him worked best—namely, Facebook.

Thierry calls social media marketing technology the new TV advertising—a revolutionary platform that allows him to reach billions of people around the world with UBS's stories instantly. While TV allowed you—at best—to target people watching a particular show in a particular city, social media technology allows you to target the exact person you want to reach, based on where they live, what they like, where they work, what their job is, and even how much money they likely make.

While this may seem a little creepy (and it is!), this is all information that people have made publicly available to Facebook, LinkedIn, Instagram, and other platforms on which they spend hours every day. And those platforms have made it incredibly easy to reach those people with stories that they're likely to love.

And the best part is, the better these stories are, the cheaper it is to reach people with them. It often costs just a penny or less. And when you have smart analytics that tell you which channels work best with which stories, you can make smart decisions about where to reach people.

Very quickly, we're seeing digital advertising become the dominant way that businesses reach the people they care about, with social media marketing technology leading the way. In late 2016, digital advertising surpassed TV advertising for the first time. And that gap will only continue to grow.

We can't tell you exactly what will work two or three years for now. But we can tell you that the killer equation for the future is breakthrough stories + smart technology to spread those stories. And the storytellers that embrace that equation are the ones who will win.

Optimize

Throughout this book, we've talked about how to use smart data and insights to make your stories better. In truth, *optimizing* isn't something that great storytellers sit down and do once a month. It's something that they're always doing. They're always looking to make things better, to get an edge.

And so, we'd like to tell you about how the impact storytelling technology had on one of us.

This is the story of how it saved Joe's career.

This story starts with a secret: Joe's a very disorganized person.

He's heard this since kindergarten. "You're going to have to learn to organize your stuff better if you're going to make it in the first grade," his first-grade teacher, Miss Jessica, told him. Her eyes lingered on his half-open backpack, stuffed with color-by-number worksheets, cracked crayons, and dry elbow pasta, which was garnished with a bursting bottle of Elmer's glue.

But he was a bright kid, so he beat the odds and made it through first grade. It took him longer than anyone else to find his stuff, sure, but he always compensated by getting his work done quickly. Each year, the warnings from his teachers continued—you'll never make it in second grade, third grade, middle school, high school—but he survived.

He then chose a small liberal arts college, Sarah Lawrence, which was the kind of place where you were never the only one with sticky elbow pasta on your notebook. Using a jack-o'-lantern bucket as a backpack was all part of the creative process on campus. He thrived. He wrote constantly and developed a couple of columns for his college newspaper. He broke some big stories, too. At the end of freshman year, he was named editor in chief.

And that's when it turned out all of his teachers were right.

Running a publication is a marathon of organization—hiring, budgeting, scheduling. Getting drafts to and from writers and editors. Making sure stories fit into the paper's layout. Joe started his tenure as editor in chief pumped up, recruiting writers with speeches he stole from *Friday Night Lights*'s coach Eric Taylor. "Clear eyes, full hearts, break stories!" didn't exactly have the same ring to it, but it worked well enough in the beginning.

But a few weeks later, he was drowning in the vast, confounding ocean of his own email account. Signing in gave him the pangs of a mild panic attack. His messy life no longer seemed so glamorous. Each week, he'd stumble into the newspaper office at 7 a.m. on a Friday and stumble out at midnight on Sunday when the issue had finally shipped. Rather than figure out a killer organizational system, he'd chosen to just simplify the process by doing everything himself. He didn't sleep much, but he survived. Just barely.

He passed the torch when he left to study abroad, but after graduation, he was back at it again as editor in chief of a digital news site he'd helped start out of a coffee shop in Brooklyn's Park Slope. While he'd been in denial throughout his childhood that his disorganization was an issue, he was fully aware of it by then. He had the sick feeling of lacking some fundamental skill, which put a hard ceiling on his potential as an editor. Instead of focusing on what he was good at—writing, editing, coming up with content strategies and creative ideas—

he spent half his time wondering, "Where the hell is that thing?" while combing through email threads.

He wishes he could say he met some guru who taught him to eat, pray, and organize. But really, he overcame his biggest flaw by falling in love with a piece of software.

Joe first found out about Contently while covering Techstars, a New York City incubator. Contently's founders were building a platform to give brands access to publishing tools and thousands of freelancers. Joe got in touch with Shane, one of the cofounders, and came on board as two of Contently's first freelance managing editors.

Most startups don't work out, and at first, Joe thought his affair with Contently would be a fling. But then the platform's calendar, text editor, and workflow sucked him in. All of his stories and assignments were in one place. He was organized. He felt like Laney Boggs in *She's All That*, suddenly transformed.

He could track when deadlines were approaching, who had worked on a particular story, and what changes they made. He had a beautiful analytics dashboard that told him what content performed best. Most importantly, he could focus on the work instead of digging through his email.

In 2013, Joe became Contently's editor in chief. For the first time, he wasn't terrified of his shortcomings. The only person scared was his therapist, who began to suspect that he'd developed romantic feelings for a content marketing software product. But working with a clear head helped him grow Contently's audience from 14,000 readers to more than 400,000.

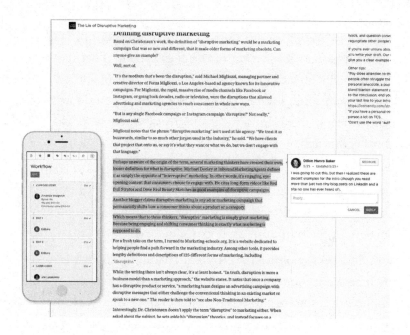

A few years ago, he could barely see the connection between software and content planning. Now he's convinced they're intrinsically linked.

We spend a lot of time thinking about the challenges marketers face. As a discipline, content marketing is new. It's hard to explain and harder to measure. Most programs are woefully understaffed.

The logical solution is content teams need more resources, but there's a chicken-and-egg dynamic. Content teams struggle to justify full-time hires until they show results, which leaves a lot of business storytellers stuck in a no-win situation.

It doesn't have to be this way. Storytelling for business is more of a quality game than a quantity game. As we've mentioned earlier in this book, the top 5 percent of branded content garners 90 percent of the engagement. That means giant media operations cranking out hundreds of stories a day won't necessarily succeed. More importantly, you do need talented people freed up to focus on great creative work that breaks through.

As a result, we think we're going to see a trend of content marketing creatives taking a new approach in the future: Instead of trying to scale their teams, they'll push for tools that maximize the output of their existing talent.

The beauty of modern content technology is that it can reduce the amount of time editors deal with busywork. We use Contently's software to receive pitches from our writers, quickly create assignments, and organize our calendar with a drag-and-drop function. From there, the platform does the rest, such as automatically paying writers when they submit a first draft, tracking revisions, and identifying passive voice and broken links. We use Contently to instantly transfer stories to WordPress so we don't have to waste time copying and pasting. And our proprietary analytics serves up cards that deliver actionable insights on metrics such as traffic, engagement, and conversions. Instead of spending hours pulling these data, we digest it in seconds.

With the right software, these operational tasks can go from occupying 50+ percent of your time as an editor to just 10 percent. In other words, you can increase your production fivefold for the price of hiring a junior editor. The folks that figure out how to do this will have a leg up in the future, free to tackle the ambitious creative projects that get noticed.

As a kid, Joe never understood why his teachers were so obsessed with organization, but now he gets it. They wanted him to spend more time being creative. Whether you're a disorganized mess like Joe, the right combination of content technology can serve as your magic binder. Whether you choose to use Contently, the point is the same: To be on top, you need to embrace your inner Lisa Frank.

8 The Storytelling Habit

Do you want to make a billion dollars? We'll tell you how. Invent a drug that builds and sculpts every muscle in your body perfectly in one dose. One pill, and you'll look like Arnold Schwarzenegger or Jillian Michaels.

If only it were that easy. The unfortunate reality of exercise is that even if you use steroids, you're going to have to make working out a habit.

Storytelling is no different. Sure, you can change people's minds with one story. You can reword a beggar's sign and get people to give more money. But if you want to build a long-term relationship—as a business or in everyday life—you're going to need to think of storytelling like going to the gym.

Every story you tell becomes a part of your overarching story. Just like every workout at the gym helps build your physique over time. The best companies are adept at consistently telling their story in a variety of ways over time. The most intriguing people tell lots of stories. They answer questions with stories. They relate to people with stories instead of just saying, "Me too."

If you've made it this far, you're probably convinced that you should be using stories more to build relationships. But it's not always easy to convince an entire organization to start going to the gym, so to speak.

In this last section of the book, we'd like to lay out a few specific ideas for how you can make the case for stories inside your company.

Selling Storytelling Inside Your Organization

Ten years ago, it was possible for one person to make content work for an entire organization. That's no longer the case. Today, you need real support internally. It won't necessarily happen all at once, but it's the first step you have to take. And while it's not easy, it pays off.

Let's look at how Marriott's content marketing program got started. Nine years ago, Kathleen Matthews, the hotel giant's executive vice president of communications, walked into Bill Marriott's office with an idea. She'd spent 25 years as a reporter and news anchor for an ABC News affiliate in Washington, DC, and she knew the power of a good story. Especially when it came from a compelling figure.

She wanted Marriott to have a blog. And she wanted Bill Marriott to write it.

"Why the heck would anyone want to read a blog from me?" Marriott, then 76 years old, responded.

Matthews quickly convinced Marriott he was the best person to tell the company's story, even though he didn't even use a computer. So they struck a compromise. Marriott would dictate a blog post once a week.

And so, Marriott's digital storytelling journey began. It started with those simple blog posts, but over the next seven years, their efforts grew exponentially. Before long, they were operating a full-fledged global media company.

In the next three years, Marriott launched a popular digital travel magazine, *Marriott Traveler*, that covers cities from Seattle to Seoul. It has built content studios on five different continents. And it's even won Emmys for its short films like *Two Bellman* and *French Kiss*.

When you walk into the ground floor of Marriott's headquarters, it fittingly looks like the lobby of a modern hotel. There are chic white lounges and cozy pods. A friendly receptionist welcomes you. But then you notice something unexpected. In the middle of the lobby, there are nine flashing screens encased in glass walls, like a TV control room that's been teleported from Hollywood to Bethesda, Maryland.

In a way, it has. Inside the control room—dubbed "M Live"—typically sit various media veterans tasked with seeing just how much a hotel brand could capitalize on the new opportunities digital media gave Marriott to tell their story.

"We are a media company now," Emmy-winner David Beebe, then Marriott's vice president of global creative, told us.[1]

It's a big statement, but one that Marriott's content production backs up. Which raises the question: How did Marriott evolve from a single woman—Kathleen Matthews—storming into the CEO's office and advocating for content to one of the most advanced content marketing operations in the world?

Well, fter a few years, Bill Marriott's blog took off. And before long, he was convinced that content was the answer to the challenges Marriott faced in telling the story of a company that spanned almost two dozen different hotel brands.

So in 2013, Marriott made a big bet and hired Karin Timpone away from the Walt Disney Company, where she had led the launch of successful digital products like WATCH

ABC, so she could connect Marriott to the "next generation of travelers." In June 2014, Beebe, who was also working for Disney, followed Timpone.

Beebe and Timpone got to work fast. By early 2015, Marriott had created a successful TV show, *The Navigator Live*; a hit short film, *Two Bellmen*; a personalized online travel magazine; and some exciting forays into virtual reality with Oculus Rift. These projects generated immediate returns, from high viewer engagement to millions of dollars in direct revenue and even content-licensing deals. They helped the company build stronger relationships with its customers.

"We've said it before—we have a very intimate relationship with our customers," Beebe said. "They sleep with us, after all. It's sort of a joke, but it's true."[2]

After these initial wins, the company doubled down on storytelling even more and beefed up its in-house staff, bringing in folks from CBS, *Variety*, and other media powerhouses.

They also joined forces with a wide range of outside creators—(including Contently!)—from famed producers Ian Sander and Kim Moses to YouTube celebrity Taryn Southern, who stars in a web series called *Do Not Disturb* in which she interviews celebrities in their hotel rooms.

Beebe rejected the temptation to insert any overt Marriott branding. When he got the first cut back from Marriott's wonderful short film, *Two Bellmen*, for instance, his first note was to take out most of the brand plugs.

"We don't want to see any 'Welcome to the JW Marriott, here's your keycard,' and then a close-up of the logo," he said. "None of that."[3]

In other words, Marriott bet on having career story-tellers lead their content marketing program—not career marketers.

The key to making this work, however, wasn't by shutting marketing out. Instead, Marriott found success by breaking down silos and gathering marketers and content people around a common cause.

The key to that is M Live, its glass-encased content studio.

Launched in October 2015, the studio has nine screens showing everything from the social media campaigns of Marriott's 19 brands to real-time booking information to Marriott's editorial calendar. But what might be even more impressive—and instructive for other brands—are the eight swivel chairs. Each seat in the glass room represents a different department such as PR/Comms, Social Media, Buzz Market-ing, Creative + Content, and even one for MEC, a media-buying agency that amplifies well-performing content at a moment's notice.

Some marketers may dismiss this scene as a fad—a foolish brand playing media company. But in truth, it's actually the sign of a great storytelling culture—one that embraces media as marketing.

At the time of this writing, although Marriott is very much building a media business—with plans to license short films and webisodes to places like Yahoo!, AOL, Hulu, Netflix, and Amazon—M Live and the Marriott Content Studio are still very much a marketing initiative.

"We did not get this far by saying, 'I want to build a media company,'" Beebe said. "First and foremost, [the goal] is to engage consumers. Get them to associate with our brands, build lifetime value with them. Content's a great way to do that."[4]

A Culture of Storytelling

While M Live and the Marriott Content Studio are making great strides reaching people externally, they're also having an impact on life inside the company. The content team has put in hard work evangelizing and explaining what they're doing—part of the reason they built M Live smack in the middle of the lobby for all to see.

One executive, for instance, spent three months leading a project to create a guide that explains M Live and how anyone in the company can help if they have an idea or see a trending story. They've connected the M Live team to customer care to handle any complaints or problems, and each Marriott brand is getting deeply involved with the content creation process. "People are getting it," Beebe said. "Now that we've done a lot, they're starting to see the impact."

Even Bill Marriott comes down to see what's going on.

"He loves it, loves the idea of what we're doing," Beebe said. "He'll just come sit down and chit-chat and pick up the phone. He's actually gotten on Matthew's computer and shown his wife stuff."[5]

It's that support from Bill Marriott and CEO Arne Sorenson that's pushed the ambitious content operation forward so it can keep transforming the company.

"That's really what our goal is," Beebe said. "To take all the brand marketers, all the brand leaders and teams, and turn them into great storytellers."[6]

Not every company needs to build a sophisticated content studio like Marriott to build a great culture of storytelling, but if they want to succeed as storytellers in the future, they do need to embrace what that studio represents—the destruction of silos and the shared goal of using stories to build relationships and make people care.

Which is, of course, what this is all about.

May the Story Force Be with You

Whether you plan to employ your new storytelling chops inside a big company like Marriott, inside a tiny marketing department at a small business, or in your own everyday work and relationships, our parting advice is the same.

It's what Ben Franklin advised more than 200 years ago:

"Either write something worth reading or do something worth writing about."[7]

Whichever you choose, we look forward to your stories.

NOTES

Chapter 1

1. Nathaniel Philbrick, *In the Heart of the Sea: The Tragedy of the Whaleship Essex*, (New York: Viking, 2000), pp xi-xii.

2. Delia Baskerville, "Developing Cohesion and Building Positive Relationships through Storytelling in a Culturally Diverse New Zealand Classroom", in *Teaching and Teacher Education*, 27:1 (2011): 107-115, https://www.sciencedirect.com/science/article/pii/S0742051X10001204.

Chapter 3

1. Benjamin Franklin, *The Autobiography of Benjamin Franklin*, (New York: E. P. Dutton & Co., 1913), pp. 18-19.

2. Ibid.

3. Ibid.

4. Ibid.

5. Ibid.

6. Ibid.

Chapter 4

1. Linda Boff, interview with Joe Lazauskas, April 2016.

2. Melissa Lafsky Wall, interview with Joe Lazauskas, February 2015.

3. Greg Cooper, keynote address at SXSW, 2016.

4. Linda Boff, interview with Joe Lazauskas, April 2016.

5. Rand Fishkin, interview with Joe Lazauskas, February 2015.

6. Jordan Teicher, "The Best Content Marketing of 2016", *The Content Strategist*, Dec 20, 2016, https://contently.com/strategist/2016/12/20/best-content-marketing-2016/.

7. Jing Cao and Melissa Mittelman, "Why Unilever Really Bought Dollar Shave Club", *Bloomberg*, July 20, 2016, https://www.bloomberg.com/news/articles/2016-07-20/why-unilever-really-bought-dollar-shave-club.

Chapter 8

1. David Beebe, interview with Joe Lazauskas, November 2015.

2. Ibid.

3. Ibid.

4. Ibid.

5. Ibid.

6. Ibid.

7. Benjamin Franklin, *Poor Richard, An Almanack For the Year of Christ 1738, Being the Second after Leap Year* (*Poor Richard's Almanac*), (Philadelphia, PA: Author, 1738).

INDEX